Report of a Study of Sexually Abused Children and Adolescents and Young Perpetrators of Sexual Abuse who were Treated in Voluntary Agency Community Facilities

ELIZABETH MONCK
MICHELLE NEW

Studies in Child Protection

LONDON: HMSO

ISBN 0 11 321926 1

Complementary Studies also available from HMSO Books include:

Parental Perspectives in Cases of Suspected Child Abuse
Hedy Cleaver and Pam Freeman (The Dartington Team)
HMSO 1995. ISBN 0 11 321786 2

Child Protection Practice: Private Risks and Public Remedies
Elaine Farmer and Morag Owen (The University of Bristol Team)
HMSO 1995. ISBN 0 11 321787 0

The Prevalence of Child Sexual Abuse in Britain
Deborah Ghate and Liz Spencer (Social and Community Planning Research)
HMSO 1995. ISBN 0 11 321783 8

Development After Physical Abuse in Early Childhood: A Follow-Up Study of Children on Protective Registers
Jane Gibbons, Bernard Gallagher, Caroline Bell and David Gordon (University of East Anglia)
HMSO 1995. ISBN 0 11 321790 0

Inter-agency Coordination and Child Protection
Christine Hallett (The University of Stirling)
HMSO 1995. ISBN 0 11 321789 7

Working Together in Child Protection
Elizabeth Birchall (The University of Stirling)
HMSO 1995. ISBN 0 11 321830 3

Paternalism or Partnership? Family Involvement in the Child Protection Process
June Thoburn, Ann Lewis and David Shemmings (University of East Anglia)
HMSO 1995. ISBN 0 11 321788 9

Operating the Child Protection System
Jane Gibbons, Sue Conroy and Caroline Bell (University of East Anglia)
HMSO 1995. ISBN 0 11 321785 4

Messages from Research
Summary
HMSO 1995. ISBN 0 11 321781 1

Acknowledgements

This research project was supported by the Department of Health.

We are grateful for the advice and support of the members of the Advisory Committee, which was chaired by Dr Stephen Wolkind.

We are also grateful for on-site advice from Dr Arnon Bentovim, Hospital for Sick Children NHS Trust. Professor June Thoburn provided helpful comments on the final draft.

We are particularly pleased to be able to acknowledge the practical help which we had for the last year of the study from Sandy Frangoulis.

In the course of this work we have met many professionals in the voluntary agencies and the centres run by the voluntary agencies, who gave their support to the research project. We had many stimulating meetings with those on whom the work depended, including the centre administrators who carried much of the burden of ensuring that questionnaires and schedules were completed and despatched to us. We are very grateful to all those who gave up time to further the aims of this study. We wish them well in the difficult work they do with abused children and young perpetrators.

We are also happy to acknowledge the help we received from several part-time staff and consultants: Maria Clement (NSPCC), Alice Stevenson and David New, and the computing advice we had from Suzanne Gauthier (Institute of Child Health).

Finally, we are very grateful to the children, young people and their parents who agreed to become part of the study population, and to those teachers who filled in the forms on their pupils.

Contents

List of Tables

List of Figures

Preface

In 1991 the Department of Health asked the Behavioural Sciences Unit, Institute of Child Health, to develop a research proposal for collaborating with various voluntary agencies in following up the progress of children referred to specialist clinics for two specific reasons. The first group was those children who had been referred after the discovery of their sexual victimisation. The second group was young people who had been referred as perpetrators of sexual abuse against others.

In previous years the Department had allocated considerable funds to several voluntary agencies which were developing treatment programmes specifically addressing the needs of these two groups of children and adolescents. The voluntary organisations, in accepting the Department of Health funds to assist this work, agreed to participate in evaluating the programmes. At the same time The National Children's Homes (NCH), while receiving government funds, also committed some of their own funds to providing specialist centres and joining the evaluation exercise.

This Report describes the development of the evaluation programme, the choice of centres which took part, the measures used to follow the progress of the children and the results. The conclusion draws on the study results to make some recommendations about the ways in which individual services could improve the evaluation of their work, and contribute at the same time to a better understanding of the long-term outcome for sexually abused children who enter treatment programmes.

We have structured the Report to make it possible to choose to read about the results from only one of the study populations. After the introduction in Chapter 1, Chapters 2 and 3 cover the aims, method and measures which are common to both study populations. Chapter 4 describes the characteristics of the two sample in considerable detail: Part 1 for the abused children, and Part 2 for the young perpetrators, and these can be read separately. Chapter 5 briefly discusses some of the differences between the two samples. In Chapter 6 we describe the results of the outcome study, again divided into two parts on the abused children and the young perpetrators. Chapter 7 presents the results of lengthy discussions with some of the Centre managers and some team members, who were involved in the study. In Chapter 8 the studies are discussed and Chapter 9 gives our conclusions and recommendations.

Summary

The aim of this study was to track the progress of two groups of children and adolescents through specialised treatment delivered in local voluntary agency centres.

In the first group, 239 sexually abused children aged between 4 and 18 years were assessed at referral for their behavioural and psychopathological needs. The ratio of boys to girls was 3:1; more than a third of the perpetrators were fathers; 60% had experienced penetrative abuse, and this was more likely from closer relatives. By referral, nearly half the children lived with lone mothers, but this represented considerable change from the position at abuse. Self-report (for the over 8s) and parental reports found high levels of depression, significantly related to penetrative experiences. For 60 children, information on progress through treatment was available. Self-esteem and depression of some, but not all, children improved. Therapists estimated that parents' own needs had diminished during treatment, and parental self-esteem improved, but other standardised and clinically generated measures showed little change.

The second group consisted of 55 young male sex offenders, assessed at referral by parental and self-report. Half these boys had experienced previous victimisation, and 40% had spent long periods away from their biological parents. The largest category of victims was siblings, and abusive actions ranged from exhibitionism to rape. Age and severity were unrelated. As a group, the boys were not significantly depressed; given the nature of their offenses, remarkably few behavioural or psychopathological needs were identified at referral. By the end of treatment, few changes were observed in behaviour or psychopathology.

The study was handicapped by the fact that information from therapists was missing for a large number of children, both at referral and at later points in the study. Sometimes this was because children had not completed their programme of therapy. The results and the difficulties of the study are discussed in detail and recommendations put forward for therapists to develop more effective ways of monitoring their own treatment and intervention programmes.

Chapter 1

Introduction and Background to the Study

Incidence, Prevalence and Pathways to Treatment

Sexually abused children and adolescents

For some years, the numbers of children and teenages who have been referred to the UK child protection services after the discovery or disclosure of their sexual victimisation has risen quite markedly. National figures are hard to obtain, but the records of children on the At Risk Registers kept by the National Society for the Prevention of Cruelty to Children (NSPCC) for nearly 20 years show that the rate of sexual abuse rose sharply in the 1980s (Creighton & Noyes, 1989). The latest NSPCC figures suggest a flattening off in this increase but overall numbers remain substantial (Creighton, 1992, Figure 7, p.64). Since the figures are probably affected by such issues as professional attitudes and alertness to the signs of abuse, both the rise and the apparent recent slowing down need to be approached with care.

In the nature of the case, it is very difficult to establish the numbers of children who experience sexual abuse in any one period (Baker & Duncan, 1985). Kelly et al. (1995) found that in a group of 16–21 year-olds as many as one half of young women and one quarter of young men had experienced some type of sexually abusive action by others before reaching the age of 18 years: the exact proportions were heavily dependent on the definitions of 'abusive'.

After disclosure or discovery of sexual abuse, it appears that some families try to deal with the issue by themselves (Briere, 1992), but it seems likely that the majority of cases become known or are already known to child protection agencies (in the UK—the NSPCC or local authority social services departments), and/or the police (Sharland et al, in press).

Some of these cases will later be passed to specialist teams of social workers, or mental health teams for assessment and therapeutic work with the abused child and his or her family; in the US Chapman & Smith (1987) have estimated that between 44% and 73% of known cases will progress to this stage. Some of these individuals or families will remain in therapy, and some will drop out. Thus, at each stage in the disclosure and treatment of sexual abuse of children there is attrition of cases (Figure 1 presents this schematically). Similar figures for sexual abuse cases are not available for the UK, but the work of Gibbons et al (1995) shows that, among child protection cases dealt with by social services departments large numbers of children were drawn into the child protection system whose needs were then not being appropriately met once it was established that protection, per se, was not needed (Department of Health, 1995).

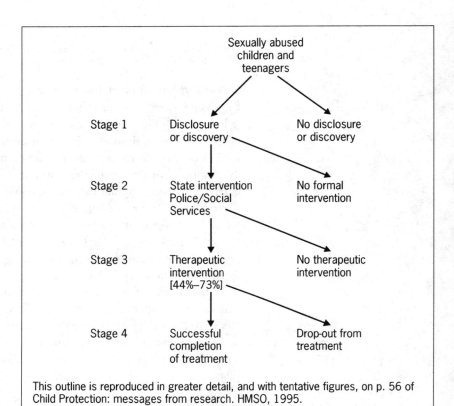

Figure 1

The route to completed treatment for sexually abused children and adolescents

Sexually abused children and teenagers

Stage 1 — Disclosure or discovery / No disclosure or discovery

Stage 2 — State intervention Police/Social Services / No formal intervention

Stage 3 — Therapeutic intervention [44%–73%] / No therapeutic intervention

Stage 4 — Successful completion of treatment / Drop-out from treatment

This outline is reproduced in greater detail, and with tentative figures, on p. 56 of Child Protection: messages from research. HMSO, 1995.

By definition, the proportion of cases which remain undisclosed is not known; Mullen et al (1993) found that only 37% of adult women recalling childhood sexual abuse had disclosed within a year, and only 7.5% had disclosed to any form of social agency. Unfortunately it is also true that the proportion of known cases of sexual abuse who do not receive treatment and the reasons for this is not known. In addition, the numbers failing to complete the therapeutic programmes they enrol on are seldom reported in the literature (Finkelhor & Berliner, 1995). In finding that only a minority of cases are provided with treatment is not unique to sexual abuse victims: for example, it appears that only a minority of depressed teenage girls are in contact with appropriate services (Cooper & Goodyer, 1993).

Even when cases are discovered it appears that, at least in some areas of the UK, three-quarters of child protection referrals drop out of the system before they reach the case conference stage or the 'at risk' register (Giller, Gormley & Williams, 1992).

Finkelhor & Berliner (1995) point out that the children in treatment are likely to be very different from those not in treatment, although there may be no one source of bias. Sharland et al (in press) noted that there was little relationship between the identified needs of children and parents at the point of disclosure or investigation, and the certainty of receiving support from local services. The important conclusion which must be drawn is that those who enter therapeutic programmes will be a very diverse group, with different experiences, different reactions, and different potential for improvement: children are in treatment because of their experience not because of their outstanding needs (Finkelhor & Berliner, 1995).

Sexually abused children are more likely to emerge from families which have a range of problems, and families in which one or both parents are absent for long periods (Russell, 1986), or levels of conflict are high (Alexander & Lupfer, 1987). It is, however, recognised that a high proportion of such families are already in touch with statutory child care agencies for other reasons, and that the effect of this is that any allegations will be more readily investigated or believed.

Young perpetrators

Acceptance that teenagers are responsible for much of the abuse of children and other teenagers has been a late development in the field of sexual abuse (reviewed by Vizard, Monck & Misch, 1995). Although published studies specifically reporting incidence or prevalence of teenage sexual abusers are rare, evidence of the likely size of the problem can be gleaned from other sources. Taken together, the evidence is remarkably consistent that this is a significant group of child abusers. Figures from the Home Office (1992) showed that 30% of sex offenders were under 21 years; information from retrospective studies of adult victims abused in childhood or 'teens suggested that more than one third of the offenders were teenagers (e.g., Finkelhor, 1979), and the Northern Ireland Child Sexual Abuse Study (Research Team, 1990) showed that 36% of the reported incidents had involved a teenager abuser. In a UK community sample of 16 to 21-year olds, Kelly et al (1995) found that, among those reporting childhood abuse, 27% of perpetrators were 13–17 years old and a further 1% were under 13 years. Gomes-Schwartz et al (1990) found one third of abusers of a clinic sample of children were teenagers. Perhaps the most important study of the prevalence of young perpetrators in the UK has come from the work of Glasgow, Horne, Calam & Cox (1994). All cases of child sexual abuse in one large city were recorded, and in one third of cases (52/155) the perpetrator was under 18 years. The authors emphasise the importance of developmental differences in the young perpetrators, and divided the sample into three age-groups: up to 7 years,

8–12 years, and 13–17 years. Comparing the ages of all sexual offenders in the sample showed that there was a very marked peak in the 13–17 year-old age group.

The importance of acknowledging that teenagers (boys and girls) are involved in sexually abusing others lies not just in the damage done to others by their current behaviour. It is clear that early offending is associated with later offending: for example, Abel et al (1987) found that over 50% of non-incarcerated para-philiacs had started abusing children while still in their 'teens. Treatment centres were developing programmes to work with this group of young people, but very little follow-up or outcome studies had been organised in the UK (NCH, 1992).

The seriousness of the sexual offenses of young perpetrators has recently been recognised by a change in the UK law on sexual offenses by younger teenagers. The Sexual Offenses Act 1993 abolished the presumption that boys aged between 10 and 13 years are incapable of vaginal or anal penetration, and therefore cannot be charged with rape.

In parallel with this changing perception of sexual offending in teenagers, has come a rise in the number of units offering specialist therapies. Knopp et al (1992) reported that, in the six years from 1986 to 1992, treatment programmes in the US had risen from 346 to 755. In only a small number of instances are outcome figures available from these programmes (Knopp et al, 1992). Several large UK children's charities as well as probation and health services, for example, now offer specialist treatment programmes. However, the efficacy of these programmes has still to be established.

When we apply the same model as we give in Figure 1 to young perpetrators of sexual offenses, a very similar picture emerges. Again, by definition, the numbers of undiscovered offenders is not known, but at each level of intervention, attrition or diversion into non-therapeutic programmes reduces the numbers who will eventually reach therapeutic intervention. Preliminary findings from a study of the progress of child abuse cases through the UK judicial system, showed that there were no mechanisms in place to identify and track discovered cases systematically (Plotkinoff & Woolfson, 1994).

Review of Treatment Outcomes

Treatment outcome for sexually abused children

There are a large number of studies of the characteristics of sexually abused children and adolescents at the time of discovery or referral to specialist child care agencies (reviewed by Kendall-Tackett et al 1993). By contrast, and despite a considerable increase in the number of specialist treatment programmes available both for sexually abused and abusive children, the efficacy of treatment programmes for sexually abused children has received remarkably little systematic attention (reviewed by Kendall–Tackett et al. 1993). In particular there is a paucity of long-term prospective outcome studies which has led to unacceptable reliance on retrospective studies for estimates of long-term harm to victims. It should be noted that this is not unusual in the literature of child psychology and psychiatry (Stevenson, 1986): a straw-poll of papers published by one leading UK journal specialising in child psychology[1] produced only thirteen papers on treatment effectiveness between 1978 and 1983.

Comparing the results of the few outcome studies in child sexual abuse poses particular problems because of the wide variation in the characteristics of the treated populations, and in the content and length of the programmes. Such studies as there are have tended to imply that any change in the status of the child (either for better or worse) is the effect of treatment. In fact, change may well be affected by other factors in the child's life, including obtaining treatment outside the study facility or the simple passage of time. Comparison is made more difficult by the wide range of measures used to assess the children and family members as they enter and leave treatment, and variable lengths of follow-up. This complex field has been carefully reviewed by Finkelhor & Berliner (1995).

Seven studies reviewed by Kendall–Tackett et al. (1993) suggested that abused children's symptoms reduced over time, and four studies are selected for presentation here. Bentovim et al. (1988) asked community social workers to report the current situation for xx children treated between 2 and 7 years previously: 61% said the children were 'better', but this leaves 39% who were presumably 'not better'. Hewitt & Friedrich (1991) found that 65% of pre-school children improved over the year following treatment.

Gomes-Schwartz and her colleagues (1990) followed up 156 boys and girls with a mean age of 10.1 years at the time of referral to a specialist sexual abuse clinic. The children were assessed at the start of treatment and again after 18 months using an inventory of behaviour problems (the Louisville Behavior Checklist), two self-esteem questionnaires (Piers-Harris and Purdue Self-concept Scales), and a symptom checklist (Child & Adolescent Behavior Checklists—developed by the Children's Hospital National Medical Center, Washington, DC). In this study 15% of subjects showed substantial recovery over 18 months, and these were the children who had received specialized treatment from the researchers. The 20% who received community-based treatment did not show the same high levels of recovery. Children who were initially asymptomatic were most likely to develop problems, and those who were most disturbed at entry to the programme tended to show improved scores. The authors point out that these results may have been statistical

---

[1] Journal of Child Psychology & Psychiatry.

artifacts: that is to say, it is not possible for a child with few or no symptoms to 'improve' to a significant extent.

Freidrich et al. (1992) studied the progress of 33 sexually abused boys who followed two treatment programmes (9 other boys did not complete the programme): for 19 boys treatment was primarily delivered in groups and for 14 treatment was primarily in individual sessions. The boys did not report improvement in depressive feelings or self-esteem, but sexualized behaviour was significantly reduced and behaviour scores improved. There was no difference in outcome by treatment modality.

Most recently, in the UK, Monck, Sharland, Bentovim et al (1995) studied the outcome for sexually abused children who received 10–12 months treatment in a specialist hospital out-patient clinic. In this study, the 47 children were randomly allocated to receiving family treatment only or additional group work appropriate to their age. The children and their mothers (or primary carer) were interviewed on entry into treatment and again 12 months later: data were obtained on the family demography and relationships, the child's abuse experiences and current behaviour. Mothers and children aged 8 years or over completed self-report questionnaires on self-esteem and depressive/anxious symptomatology. Clinicians working with the families rated them on twelve family treatment aims. Judged by the standardised research measures the addition of group work did not improve outcome for the children, but did do so for their mothers. Clinical ratings at the end of treatment suggested that group work produced a better outcome on a number of family treatment aims relating both to the mothers and to the children. One explanation of these apparently conflicting results is that the clinicians were not blind (as the researchers were) to the type of treatment their patients had followed. Thus, it was possible that the personal investment of clinicians in the success of group work led to them rating patients who had taken part in groups as more successful than they really were. However, it was also clear that the ratings obtained from clinicians and research measures tapped different aspects of the child's and family's progress.

Treatment outcome studies of young sex offenders

Outcome studies of non-incarcerated young perpetrators who receive therapeutic interventions is even less frequently reported than the outcome for abused children. Several studies have been published from the United States, but these have largely been of incarcerated young sex offenders; treatment outcome studies from other countries, including the UK are rare. Most outcome studies use recidivism as the main measure of success, but other studies focus on the reduction of deviant arousal and increased impulse control (e.g., Hunter & Santos, 1990; Becker, 1990), increasing victim awareness, correcting distorted cognitions around sexuality and children, and interrupting the 'cycle of abuse'. Much of this work originated in therapies for adult male offenders, and some parts may not directly transfer to adolescents. A large number of outcome studies employ methods, such as penile plethysmographs, or sexually explicit questionnaires which are not appropriate for the sort of community-based treatment setting included in the present study (e.g. Becker, Kaplan & Kavoussi, 1988; Murphy et al. 199). The work on testing sexual fantasies in adult offenders is almost impossible to replicate with youngsters, not least for ethical reasons.

Work with adolescent sex offenders should include attending to peer group relationships and school performance, and take account of developmental issues. Vizard, Monck & Misch (1995) have recently reviewed outcome studies for adolescent sex offenders, and concluded that there is an urgent need to develop measures of improvement for this population of young offenders.

The numbers involved in outcome studies of adolescents tend to be very small (e.g., McCune, in press). It is not uncommon to find that a substantial proportion of those entering treatment either do not complete, or do not attend all sessions (Becker, 1990).

Chapter 2

Aims and Methodology

Aims and Hypotheses

The study was set up to track the progress made by children and adolescents who had been sexually abused through the treatment programmes they attended in their locality. The aim was the same for the young perpetrators of sexual offenses against children. The participating treatment centres were almost all organised by voluntary agencies, rather than by the NHS or the local department of Social Services; many, however, worked in close collaboration with local Social Service Departments (SSDs), and some employed NHS psychiatrists and psychologists as consultants.

Among the abused children it was predicted that the severity of the abuse experience would be reflected in more symptomatology at the start of treatment, and a less positive response to the therapy. Among the young perpetrators we expected to find more behaviour problems and other symptoms in those with a history of more severe abusive behaviour. When such abusive behaviour had been more serious and been of longer duration we expected to find a less positive response to the treatment programmes.

It is worth pointing out at this stage that the research project was not planned to test whether particular treatment programmes were more likely to be associated with greater improvement in the abused children or young perpetrators. This decision was based on two factors. First, the treatment centres were expected to be delivering quite varied, eclectic programmes. They were not chosen to represent particular treatment modalities or perspectives. Second, the numbers of children attending any one type of treatment programme (or treatment centre) was unlikely to be large enough to test any treatment hypothesis.

The fact that treatment programmes were likely to (and in the event were found to) vary between centres might be thought to undermine the value of looking at outcome. However, there is an argument for accepting that clinical judgment leads to the 'best' or most appropriate treatment being chosen for each child or adolescent. Testing the outcome is in effect testing the most appropriate treatment, while retaining the value and independence of professionals' judgment.

Selection of the treatment centres

The centres are run by a number of different voluntary organisations: the National Society for the Prevention of Cruelty to Children (NSPCC), the Family Service Units (FSU), the St Christopher's Fellowship, the National

Children's Homes (NCH) and the Northorpe Hall Trust. Funds from the Department of Health for developing this treatment work were routed through the head offices of each organisation. Each organisation then selected the individual centres which they wished to see involved in the work. The two centres in Northern Ireland were selected by the NI Department of Health & Social Services. A list of the participating centres is given in Appendix A.

The Department of Health initiative carried a commitment to become involved in the monitoring programme run by the researchers at the Institute of Child Health. For staff at the centres, the commitment to monitoring outcome was thus taken externally. It is also important to note that the eighteen centres which were eventually involved in the treatment outcome work were not selected by reference to research criteria.

Selecting the Two Samples

The samples consisted of all the sexually abused children (aged 6–18 years) and all young perpetrators (aged 12–18 years) referred to the treatment centres. Both samples were drawn from among those who attended these centres between December 1991 (or whenever the centre opened after that date) and December 1993, when new cases ceased to be accepted into the study.

The distinction between the victims and young perpetrators is, in reality, not always clear. Many young perpetrators have been victims of sexual abuse, and some victims exhibit sexualized behaviour which could easily be described as abusive towards others. For purposes of this study the distinction was based on the judgment of the therapists as to whether the main focus of the referral and ensuing therapeutic work with an individual was on their victim status or their abusive actions. Inevitably, such a distinction is less than rigorous; different teams or therapists will take a different view about the focus of work with abused perpetrators or abusive victims.

Method of Data Collection

The study population was recruited, not by the research team, but by the centre workers. Centre workers were responsible for introducing the research programme, getting permission from the subjects and their parents, and asking them to complete the questionnaries. They were also responsible for filling in the data schedules on demographic and abuse information.

For this reason and in recognition that few therapists would have the specific skills and experience required for the new tasks we were asking them to take on, *Information and Training Days* were held in each centre. Initially, each centre was visited by one or both the researchers to introduce the research project and explain how the work could best be organised. These sessions combined information about the aims and methods of the research with discussion and training on certain key topics. For example, since confidentiality was a major concern, much care was taken in explaining the ways in which the ICH team would be able to guarantee anonymity on records, thus making it clear that centre workers could pass on this guarantee to each client when they asked for cooperation with the research. It was recognised that very few centre workers would have had previous experience of obtaining informed consent for research from parents and children. They were therefore encouraged to join in role play sessions explaining the project and seeking consent from 'parents' (played by colleagues) who had varying attitudes of anxiety, hostility or doubt about the value of research. Specific attention was also paid to the issue of how to 'help' someone who was a non-reader (or poor reader) to fill in the self-report questionnaires. Again it was recognised that some, but probably few, of the centre workers would have had experience in this task.

Recognising that centre workers would be asking for cooperation from local authority social service staff and schools, the senior researcher wrote to Directors of Education and of Social Services in the areas covered by the research, with an explanation of the research aims and methods, and the likely (small) impact on their staff. They were invited to contact the researchers with queries, if they had any.[2]

The centre workers were asked to obtain information on the family demography, the child's schooling and aspects of the abuse experience when the child was first referred. Further information was also to be obtained when the therapeutic intervention ended, and again, 12 months after referral.

At each of these time points the centre workers were expected to administer the self-report questionnaires to children and parents (see next chapter on Measures).

Information on the young perpetrators was collected in the same way at the same three time points.

Ethical Issues and Confidentiality

There were two major ethical issues: first, that *informed consent* should be obtained from clients, and second, that *confidentiality* should be ensured.

Centre workers were encouraged to introduce the research as an integral part of the work that they did, and to obtain signed consent from parents and older children and teenagers.[3] Each parent and consenting child was given a short description for them to keep of the research aims and what it would

---

[2] One Director of Social Services responded with some questions.
[3] Examples of the consent forms are included in Appendix C.

mean for them to enter the programme.[4] Some centres incorporated these consent forms and information forms.

Confidentiality was established by ensuring that the researchers did not know (and therefore did not record) the names of the clients. Each case was allocated a unique identification number which was recorded in the centre on the client's case notes or in a Record Book of the research sample. Records sent to the researchers did not contain the names or addresses of families.

---

[4] Examples of the Information leaflets for parents and teenagers are given in Appendix D.

Chapter 3

Measures

Introduction: Choosing what to measure

One of the most important considerations in choosing what measures to use in this field is that 'sexual abuse' is not a condition or syndrome, but an experience or set of experiences to which children's and parents' responses vary considerably. The variation in responses arises not least because there is no one 'type' of child who experiences sexual abuse.

Among young perpetrators of sexual abuse and their parents the range of current behaviour and mood disturbance also varies widely. Measures suited to monitoring the progress of young perpetrators have not received as much attention as they might, given the importance of the subject (Vizard et al. 1995). Clinical work frequently focuses on issues such as accepting responsibility for the abusive behaviour, while reliable ratings or self-report questionnaires are not yet available.

In view of this and the fact that we expected many of the young perpetrators to have been victims of abuse led us to use some of the same measures with this sample as well as the victim sample. In addition, we adapted the Blame Attribution Inventory (BAI) developed by Gudjonsson & Singh (1989) for use with adult offenders.

Standardised psychological measures were chosen which met four characteristics. First, it was important that they were relevant to the symptoms which many sexually abused children and young perpetrators were reported as showing; second, that they could be used to distinguish the symptomatic from the symptom-free child; third, that they were capable of measuring changed symptom levels; and fourth, that they were reasonably easy for children and parents to complete. We were also influenced by the fact that some measures are used very widely in the literature on sexually abused children, and comparisons with other samples would be facilitated.

Although only some of the mothers (primary carers) were expected to receive substantial support in the centres, it was recognised that they might show psychological distress and a high level of 'need' at the time of referral, which might be expected to diminish over the period of their child's treatment. It was decided, therefore, to administer self-report questionnaires on depressive and anxious states and self-esteem to the mothers at all three time points, and also to ask the centre workers to assess their outstanding 'needs' (see below).

Standardised Questionnaires for Children & Adolescents

a) Children's Depression Inventory (CDI) (Kovacs & Beck, 1977). Depression is very commonly noted in sexually abused children, particularly adolescents (reviewed by Kendall-Tackett et al., 1993). The CDI presents 27 questions as groups of three sentences from which the child or young person selects the one which best describes how they have been feeling over the previous two weeks. Responses are scored 0, 1 or 2; total scores of 19 or more are regarded as placing the respondent in a group 'at risk' of depressive episode; scores between 9 and 18 (inclusive) represent 'mild depression'.

The CDI discriminates between clinical and non-clinical samples, and has been found to correlate with low self-esteem and a depressive attributional style.

b) Self-esteem: adapted from self-report questionnaires developed by Harter (1982, 1985) for use with children aged 8 years and upwards, and for adolescents. The adapted version has 45 questions covering specific domains, and incorporates the 10 questions on global self-esteem from Rosenberg's Self-esteem questionnaire (Rosenberg, 1967). The informant rates items as 'very true for me', 'quite true for me', 'not very true for me' and 'not at all true for me': these responses score 0, 1, 2, 3 with high scores indicating higher self-esteem.

c) Behaviour & adjustment: Youth Self-report (YSR) (Achenbach & Edelbrock, 1983). There are 112 pre-coded questions, which sum into eight syndrome scores; these are intended as descriptive summaries of the items in each syndrome, rather than diagnostic labels (Achenbach, 1991). Three syndrome scores (Withdrawn, Somatic complaints and Anxious/ depressed) sum to an Internalization score and two (Delinquent Behavior and Aggressive Behavior) sum to an Externalization score. Computer-derived high scores indicate pathology, but the orginators of the Child Behavior Checklist/YSR have consistently pointed out that there can be no simple cut-off point to distinguish 'normal' from 'abnormal' children.

d) Fears Schedule: [NB victims only] short form of the Fears Schedule for Children-R (Ollendick, 1993; Stevenson, Batten & Cherner, 1992). Data for 782 twins aged 8–18 years were re-analyzed using 48 items only of the original 80-item version. The shorter version is highly correlated with the previous version (r=0.96) and has good internal consistency (Cronbach's alpha=0.941). The 45 items were chosen to reflect particular fears and worries which sexually abused children are frequently reported as showing

(Smith & Bentovim, 1994). Because the number of items was reduced from 80 to 45, mean scores from the previous published studies using the longer version cannot be compared with those from the present study.

e) Blame Attribution Inventory: [NB only young perpetrators] The Sexual Abuse Blame Attribution Inventory was derived by New & Monck from the revised Blame Attribution Inventory created for adult offenders (Gudjonsson & Singh, 1989; Gudjonsson & Petursson, 1991). Three factors on the BAI distinguish attribution as Internal (feelings of guilt or remorse). External (blaming (the crime on the victim, social circumstances or society), or what Gudjonsson has called 'mental element' (blaming the crime on mental illness or poor self-control). Eighteen items load on the factor of guilt, 15 on the factor of external attribution, and nine on the factor of 'mental element'. Validity and reliability for the amended version have not been established. Gudjonsson & Petursson (1991) found that, following interpersonal crimes, adults were more likely to attribute blame to mental factors operating at the time of the crime, while sexual offenders reported highest levels of remorse (internal attribution).

Standardised Questionnaires for Parents

a) The 28-item General Health Questionnaire. The GHQ was developed as a screening instrument for use in primary health-care settings (Goldberg & Hillier, 1979). Questions are scored on Likert scale (0, 1, 2, 3) to give four subscores: depressed mood, anxiety, social dysfunction and somatic symptoms. A total score is derived from re-scoring questions 0, 0, 1, 1; a cut-off point of 4/5 indicates those at risk of more severe depressed/ anxious disorders.

b) Self-esteem Inventory: derived from Messer & Harter (1986), the inventory has eight domains (body image, paid employment, caring for others, running the household, moral self, cleverness, friendship & confiding) and one measure of global self-esteem.

c) Beck Depression Inventory (BDI): unlike the GHQ, the BDI was designed for use in psychiatric populations (Beck et al. 1961; Beck & Steer, 1987). We included it in the current study because of its wide popularity in the US literature on sexual abuse, but it was not developed as a screening instrument for detecting depressive syndromes, and needs to be interpreted with caution (Beck & Steer, 1987). The questions are presented in the form of alternative statements. The respondent chooses the statement which best describes how they have been feeling in the 'past week, including today'. The 21 pre-coded items cover depressive symptomatology, scored 0, 1, 2, 3. Total scores of 0–9 indicate minimal or no depression, 10–18 mild to moderate depression, 19–29 as moderate to severe depression and scores above 30 severe depression. In 'normal' populations a BDI total score of 15 or more may indicate some depressive symptomatology.

d) Child Behavior Checklist (CBCL): this is the parents' version of the Youth Self-report described above. The CBCL has been used in a wide variety of studies of sexually abused children (e.g., Friedlander, Weiss & Taylor, 1986; Tong, Oates & McDowell, 1987).

Standardised Questionnaire for Teachers

a) Teachers' Report Form (TRF) (Achenbach, 1991): the teachers' version of the Youth Self-report and Child Behavior Checklist described above. The TRF is designed to be completed by teachers who have known the pupil in the school setting for at least two months. The form does not require specialist training to complete.

For all versions of the Child Behavior Checklist (parents', children's and teachers'), results are presented for the two key factors of Internalizing and Externalizing problem scores, as well as the total problem scores, using the most recent scoring systems (Achenbach, 1991).

A summary of these questionnaires is shown in Table 1. The questionnaires were bound into small booklets which were given to the children and young people, and their parents or parent-substitutes. The teachers' questionnaires were separately sent to the schools with a letter from the centre workers when parents and teenagers had given permission.

Young Perpetrators' Re-offending

In addition to the behavior checklists and the self-report measures, it was planned to collect information on re-offending (both sexual and non-sexual) by the young perpetrators. The single most important indicator of successful therapy remains the absence of, or the reduction in further offenses, even in the context of a limited one-year follow-up.

Practitioners' Identification of Clients' Needs

In addition to the standardised measures described above, a section was included in each child's/adolescent's schedule in which currently observed psychological symptoms and behaviour difficulties could be recorded by the therapists. Such information was intended to add a clinical dimension to the

Table 1 **Questionnaires used in the study**

Informants	Self-report [SR]	Questionnaire title
Abused children	SR	Children's Depression Inventory
Abused Children	SR	Self-esteem inventory
Abused Children	SR	Youth Self Report (from age 12)
Abused Children	SR	Fears Schedule
Young perpetrators	SR	Children's Depression Inventory
Young perpetrators	SR	Self-esteem inventory (a/a)
Young perpetrators	SR	Youth Self Report (from age 12)
Young perpetrators	SR	Blame Attribution Inventory
Parents	SR	General Health Questionnaire
Parents	SR	Beck Depression Inventory
Parents	SR	Self-esteem inventory
Parents or Carers	on the child	Child Behavior Checklist
Teachers	on the child	Child Behavior Checklist

standardised measures, and provide an opportunity for the therapist to note a wider range of relevant issues than any one standardised measure could cover. Following early discussions with some of the centre workers, the use of another standardised checklist (e.g. the Trauma Symptom Checklist) was rejected in favour of a more open format, which it was agreed would be closer to the recording style of most social workers on the teams. Therapists were asked to record their comments under 11 headings which covered the problems commonly recorded in the literature on sexually abused children (e.g., Gomes–Schwartz et al, 1990) or sexually abusive youngsters (e.g., Becker, 1990; Ryan & Lane, 1991; O'Callaghan & Print, 1994).[5] It was emphasised to the centre workers that we were interested in needs identified by them, whether or not the centre would provide a solution. For example, if the therapist knew that there were school problems we asked that they record these, even though responsibility lay with the school not the centre to sort them out.

These comments were independently rated as present or absent in 70 categories in 16 clusters by the two researchers (EM & MN); agreement was achieved on whether symptoms/needs were 'present' or 'absent' in 93% comments, and on allocation to 'categories' in 95% of comments. The sixteen clusters are given below.

---

[5] The three pages for recording outstanding 'needs' are given in Appendix B.

Table 2 **The identification of needs by centre workers**

Clusters	Component variables
Psychological Needs	Depression, anger, fear, anxiety Develop hope, optimism re future Feel emotionally secure in family Resolve ambivalent feelings towards family members
Conduct Problems	Learn to accept rules Reduce challenging behaviour Learn boundaries round behaviour Listen & take instruction
Needs in relation to Peers	To be treated as normal by peers To develop normal relationships To develop trusting relationships
Physical/Medical Needs	Needs in relation to chronic illness Bladder control/problems Bowel control/problems Paediatric referral needed
Needs in relation to Sexual Abuse Experience	To be able to talk about victimisation without fear of distress or anger in others Understand that is believed To stop denying aspects of own abuse To clarify feelings about abuser
Post-Traumatic Symptoms	Nightmares, flashbacks, hyper-arousal, etc Others need to be sensitive to PTSD To reduce avoidance of talking about abuse
Safety Needs	To feel safe in family & elsewhere Injunction needed against perpetrator Placement needs Parents need to protect victim against more abuse
School/College Needs	School performance problems Attendance problems Protection from harassment & bullying Needs specific help from teachers Reduction in own bullying behaviour
Feelings about self-worth	Build self-confidence & self-esteem Build assertiveness & social skills Learn not to blame self for abuse & consequences of abuse To know that it was right to tell
Sexuality & Sex Education	To understand how abuse might affect future sexual choices & attitudes Clarity about appropriate touching Learn/revive appropriate modesty Learn about sex between peers Sex education Learn age-appropriate sexual behaviour

Table 2 *contd*

Clusters	Component variables
Young Perpetrators: Specific needs in relation to abusive behaviour	Address cognitive distortions about sexual issues & gender issues Accept responsibility for abusive behaviour Development of empathy Reduce avoidance in talking about sexually abusive actions Understand own cycle of abuse
Needs of Siblings	Need to feel more secure Need to be investigated for abuse Need to know effects of abuse on victim
Strengths of Young Person	Has supportive parents/family Has temperamental strengths Supportive community network
Parents' Needs	To cope with anger towards perpetrator Get help with feelings: failure, guilt, hopelessness To deal with own experiences of abuse Marital/sexual counselling Psychological needs of parents
Parenting Needs	Avoid over-compensation to victim Cope with child's behaviour Trust other adults with child Parenting skills & competencies Provide positive role model for victims and young perpetrators Believe & support young person
Referral Needs	Refer on to child psychotherapists Refer to psychologists/psychiatrists
Needs in Relation to Court	Support & information about court Visit to court

Chapter 4

Results

Part 1

The Sexually Abused Children

The results are presented separately for victims of abuse and young perpetrators, although some comparisons are made between the two samples in Section V. Results for young perpetrators are given in Part 2 of this Section.

Availability of information from questionnaires and schedules

Figure 2 shows the responses which were achieved on the various questionnaires, and data schedules for the abused children at the three time points (see Chapter 2). The full range of information should have included data schedules from centre workers, self-report questionnaires for all children over 8 years, and all mothers. Where mothers were absent, the current carer should have completed the behaviour checklist on the child.

Some part of the necessary information was available for 239 children at Time 1, but complete information (from centre workers and mothers/carers and teachers and the child if they were old enough to contribute) was only available for 144. Once allowance has been made for children under 8 years who would not have been asked to fill in questionnaires, it was clear that self-report questionnaire data were missing for only 12 children over 8 years. More worrying was the fact that only 172 schedules, covering demographic and abuse information at referral, were completed by the centre workers; 67 schedules were missing. Complete self-report questionnaires were available for only 144 mothers, although 163 checklists of the children's behaviour were completed by a combination of mothers and carers.

At Time 2 some data (but not the full range) were available for only 79 children (self-report questionnaires) and 52 mothers. The centre workers provided further information on only 66 children.

Time 3 material was available from only three children, seven mothers and six centre workers and will therefore not be presented in this report.

Throughout most of this section results will be presented for 172 children on whom information was available from social workers and centre workers who completed the Time 1 data schedule (see above). In the figures given below we differentiate between the 67 cases for whom data are *missing*, and those among the remaining 172 for whom the social workers recorded that they did not have information (*not known*).

In the context of so much missing information it was important to establish whether there were any systematic biases which distinguished those cases on which we did have information from those on which we did not.

There were no differences in Children's Depression Inventory, Fears Schedule or self-esteem scores between those for whom we had the centre workers' Time 1 data schedule and those for whom we did not. With the exception of age at referral in which there was no difference it was not possible to assess whether there were any other systematic

**Figure 2
Protocols
received from
all centres
—victims**

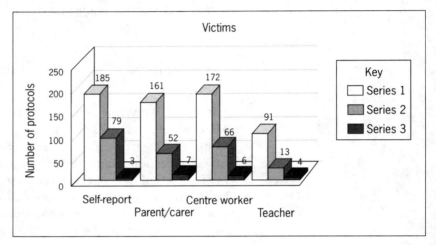

demographic differences as the specific information was not available. There were no differences in the scores on maternal self-report measures between cases for which we did or did not have demographic information.

The Demographic Characteristics of the Victims

Gender and family size

In a sample of 239 victims of sexual abuse on whom some information was collected at the start of the therapies, 185 (77%) were girls and 55 (23%) were boys. Twelve victims (7%) were only children, 44 (26%) had one sibling, and the rest (116–67%) had two or more siblings. When the subjects themselves were included in the sibling group it was apparent that the families tended to be larger than the majority in this country (Mean: 3.45: mean UK, family size: 1.8 (OPCS, 1989)).

Ethnicity

Ethnic status was reported by centre workers, and available for 172 individuals. Almost all the children were white European (93%), ten children

(6%) were reported to have mixed parentage; one child was of Afro-Caribbean parentage and one of Indian parentage.

Age

The age distribution of the victims at the time of referral to the centres was from 4 years 2 months to 17½ years, with one girl of 20 years included because her functional age was about 12 or 13 years (mean 11.08 years, median 11 years, excluding the 20-year old). The age distribution is shown in Figure 3. Boys were significantly younger than girls at referral, largely because there was an absence of victimised teenage boys (t-value=3.18, 83.9 df, p <.002), a point which has been observed in other clinic studies (e.g., Monck et al. 1995).

Figure 3
Age of victims at referral

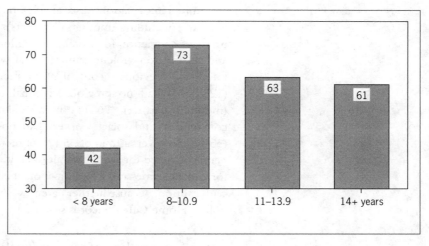

Family composition

At the time of the abuse the largest single group of children (69–41%) was living in reconstituted families, followed by the children who lived with both their own parents (61–36%). This figure might be contrasted with a sample of sexually abused children whose abuser was outside the family, where about 80% of the children lived with two biological parents (Van Scoyk, Gray & Jones, 1988).

However, by the time the children had been referred to the treatment centres there had been a considerable change in household composition. The largest number (78–45%) was now the group living with their mother alone, while only 36 (21%) lived in reconstituted families and 31 (18%) with their own parents. The remaining 16% lived in a variety of households, including a small number in children's homes.

This change of circumstance represents a considerable upheaval in many children's lives, and probably forms a particularly important aspect of the family environment in the background of therapy. From the point of view of the mothers who are still parenting the abused child it is pertinent to point out that, in addition to the new role as single parent, they face the near certainty of poverty. Information was available for 98 families on whether they were dependent on family income support at the time of referral. Out of 23 single mothers, 22 (96%) drew family income supplements compared with 35 (46%) out of 75 other households; a difference which was statistically significant (x^2=17.36, 1df, p <.0001).

In all, 158 children were living with their own mother and 147 of these mothers completed forms on their children.

Parents' criminal records

Limited information was available on the criminal records of mothers and 'fathers' (including mothers' partners). Among 172 mothers, one had previous conviction for violence to children, one for neglect of her children and six for non-violent crimes; social workers recorded that they did not know the previous record of 36 women. The large majority of mothers (128–72%) had no previous criminal convictions. Among 172 'fathers' (mother's partner), 76 (44%) were known to have had no previous convictions, and social workers had no information in another 61 cases (35%). However, a total of 35 (20%) men had previous convictions: 13 had been convicted for sexual assault of children, one for neglect of children, 14 for violent crimes and 7 for non-violent crimes. These figures must be treated with caution, because neither parent was asked for this information, nor were police/Home Office records searched.

Previous experience of abuse and neglect

Part of the background to the current abuse is the child's previous experience of abuse or neglect. Very high levels of abuse and neglect were found in the cases for which we had reports from social workers. However, even in the 172 completed records, social workers did not know what the previous abuse experiences had been of 69 children. For the remaining 103 children, 21 (20%) had experienced sexual abuse on a previous occasion. Either previously or associated with the current sexual abuse 32 children (19%) had a history of neglect, 87 (51%) had a history of emotional abuse, and 39 (23%) had a history of physical abuse.

Schooling information

Information about schooling was available for 172 children and young people. Among these, twelve children were attending special schools, although 21 children had Statements of special educational needs either completed (15) or in preparation (6) at the time of referral, suggesting that a number of children remained integrated into mainstream school despite their special needs. Only two children were recorded as having left school.

Source of referral and previous investigation of abuse

Most of the children were referred to the treatment centres by social services (136–81%). The rest of the referrals came from General Practitioners (3), child guidance (3), health visitors (2), self-referral (13), and other (12).

By the time they were referred to the treatment centres, 80 children (47% of 172 cases) had received a medical examination after the abuse was discovered or disclosed. Social workers reported that 65 children (38%) did not get a medical, and for 28 cases (16%) they had no information. Among the 80 children who received a medical examination this was said to have provided definite confirmation of sexual abuse in 36 cases (45%), doubtful confirmation in 10 cases (13%), and no direct confirmation in 31 cases (39%). Children were far more likely to receive a medical when the abuse had been penetrative, rather than non-penetrative or non-contact (x^2=16.28, 2df, p <.001), but even so, one third of the children who reported penetrative experiences did not receive a medical. Sharland et al. (in press) have also noted that receiving a medical is not clearly based on the reported abuse experience.

However, against this evidence it is worth noting that Dubowitz et al (1992) found that the medical examination of sexually abused children, along with their own disclosure, was more influential in confirming the abuse than the presence of sexualized behaviour or somatic symptoms. In the present sample, abuse can be presumed as confirmed (or else the children would not be in therapy). We cannot comment on the place of the medical in the process of confirmation, but draw attention to the association between reported experiences and the use of the medical.

Legal status of victims

The majority of the children (137–80%) were not the subject of any orders under the Children Act 1989 (Figure 4). However, fourteen (6%) were subjects of Care Orders, giving the local authority parental responsibilities in addition to the parents. A further six had Supervision orders, also placing the child under the supervision of the local authority. At the time of referral one child was the subject of an emergency protection order, which can last a maximum of fifteen days. Various orders had been made under S. 8 of the Children Act (1989):

(i) four children were subject to contact orders, which specify that the person with parental responsibility for the child must arrange for contact to be maintained by visits or staying with the person named in the order; and

(ii) two children were subject to residence orders specifying with whom the child should live.

Only 20 children were on the local child protection registers (12% of cases for which information was available). It is, of course, impossible to comment on whether this proportion would have been larger or smaller in previous years, because figures of children on the registers have not been compared with figures of children entering therapeutic programmes. Nationally, there has been a noticeable drop in the numbers on protection registers since the Children Act was implemented and the use of 'grave concern' was discouraged. However, in addition to these national trends, Gibbons and her colleagues have shown that registration is not necessarily related to levels of need, but may involve a range of other considerations (Gibbons et al, 1993). There is also some evidence that local authorities may be reducing the rate of legal proceedings in child abuse cases (Sone, 1994).

Figure 4
Legal status of the abused children at referral

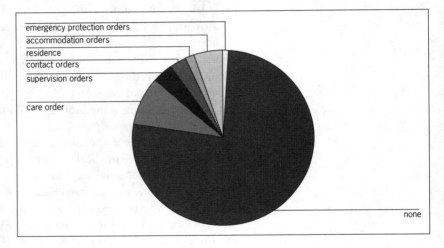

The Perpetrators

Numbers of abusers and numbers of victims

The large majority of children (133–79%) were abused by a single person, but 22 (13%) children had been abused by two people, and a further 13 by more than two people. There were no cases of ritual abuse in the sample.

Other victims were said to have been involved in 77 cases: there was a tendency for this to be more likely when the perpetrator was a parental figure ('father'), but this was not a significant difference.

Gender of perpetrators and relationship with victim

As in nearly all treated child sexual abuse samples the very large majority of known perpetrators were males (204:13 males:females—including perpetrators acting in secondary roles). Most of the female perpetrators in this sample appeared only to be acting with males, but three mothers were sole abusers. The overall relationship of the main perpetrator to the victims in the current case is shown in Figure 5. More than one third of the perpetrators were fathers or father surrogates (64/171—37%), while nearly 40% (66) were non-family, most of whom lived in the neighbourhood and were well known to the children. One quarter were other relatives (41/171—24%). Most of the latter group were friends of the family or neighbours, and only 5 were genuinely strangers.

It is the effect of the high numbers of father-figures among the perpetrators which led to the large number of mother-alone families at the time of referral which we have noted above.

**Figure 5
Relationship of perpetrator to victim**

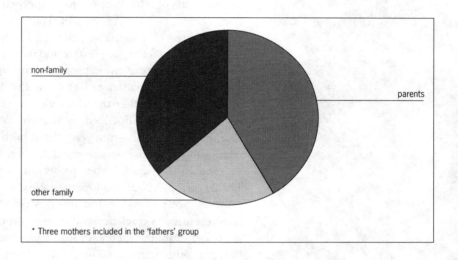

* Three mothers included in the 'fathers' group

The age of the perpetrators was recorded in 119 cases and varied from 7 to 74 years. Only 14 of these perpetrators were within five years of the victims own age and the mean difference in age was 23 years. This suggests that although there were 13 siblings, four cousins and several teenagers among the 'neighbours', that the majority of perpetrators were targeting children considerably younger than themselves.

These data emphasise that it is unwise to seek 'typical' abusers on the basis of their relationship with the child, their age, social class, previous convictions or even their gender. Perpetrators came from all parts of the family and neighbourhood, both genders, a broad age-range and from among those with few or no previous convictions for abuse of children or other crimes of personal violence. There are no simple ways to identify perpetrators in the child's community, although the importance of doing that is acknowledged (Smith, 1994).

The legal disposition of the perpetrators

The outcome was known for 203 perpetrators involved in the abuse of 164 children. Of these perpetrators, half (103—51%) were not charged, usually because there was judged to be 'insufficient evidence' for a successful prosecution. Of the remaining 100, seven (3%) had been cautioned, twenty two (11%) were on bail, 13 (6%) had probation orders, 28 (14%) were in prison and 10 (5%) were incarcerated as juveniles; 13 (6%) perpetrators had been charged but the outcome was not known, and six (3%) had been charged and acquitted. One perpetrator had committed suicide.

Thus only a very small proportion of cases moved to any form of prosecution. For half the perpetrators no legal action had occurred following the discovery or disclosure of the abuse. This figure is lower than in several other reports of what happens to the perpetrators in child sexual abuse cases. For example, Gomes-Schwartz et al (1990) found that 69% of perpetrators in cases referred to a specialist child sexual abuse clinic were not seen by the police; Sharland et al. (in press) found that only 5% of cases dealt with by one child protection team were processed through to prosecution.

Myers (1993) had noted that, in the US, decisions to prosecute are influenced by whether the child victim will be a credible witness, a view which is heavily influenced by the child's age. In the current study, the absence of any legal action was related both to the children's age and to the relationship with the perpetrator. Children were significantly more likely to be less than 10 years old when prosecutions were not pursued (t-test: t=3.18, 122.29 df, p <.002), and perpetrators were more likely to be "other" relatives, not parents or non-relatives (x^2=6.90, 2df, p. 03). On the other hand there was no relationship between the type of abuse experienced and the decision about whether or not to prosecute the offender, which had been noted in other studies (Gray, 1993; Tjaden & Thoennes, 1992). It must be emphasised that these figures relate to only 163 children out of the total of 239 cases. The 'missing' cases may have shown higher levels of active legal 'follow-through' by the authorities.

In 51 cases the perpetrator moved out of the victim's original home. In 19 of these cases the perpetrator left voluntarily; in 32 cases the perpetrator was legally forced to move. In this latter group, 19 out of 32 were fathers, 11 were other family and 2 were non-family. It is not possible to report on the numbers for which attempts to remove the perpetrator were initiated but unsuccessful. In view of the rising concern about how difficult it is to remove a perpetrator father from the family home (Cohen, 1994), the ratio of voluntary to enforced moves is interesting. In 24 cases the victims left home, either with the non-abusing parent (8 cases) or away from family (16 cases).

Abuse History

Age at onset and duration of abuse

Information about the age at onset of the abuse was available for 140 cases: the range in these cases was from 3 years to 16 years, with a mean of 8 years. For 33 children the age at onset was not known to the social workers who completed the schedule (Figure 6).

Age at cessation was also not recorded for all the 172 children the social workers reported on. Out of 145 cases on whom there was information, age

Figure 6
Age at onset of abuse

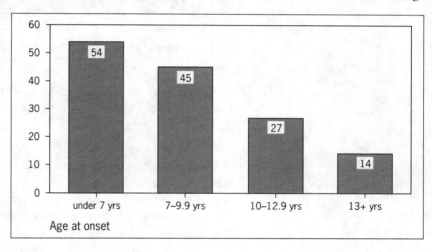

Age at onset

at the end of abuse ranged from 3 years 6 months to 16 years 6 months, with a mean of 9 years 10 months. Information missing on the children's age at the beginning and end of their abuse experience inevitably affects what is known about duration. Among 138 cases, duration ranged from less than one month to 14 years 9 months (mean: 22.6 months, SD: 29.2). For the majority of children, duration was less than 12 months (Figure 7). Duration should not be confused with other aspects of the abuse experience like frequency: for several children the abuse may have been quite infrequent, but since it had not been stopped the fear of repetition may loom as large as for children experiencing abuse repeated at very short intervals. We recognise that frequency is probably an extremely important aspect of severity, but we did not ask the social workers to record any information on frequency because it is likely to vary *within* one child's experience.

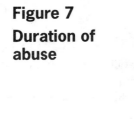

**Figure 7
Duration of
abuse**

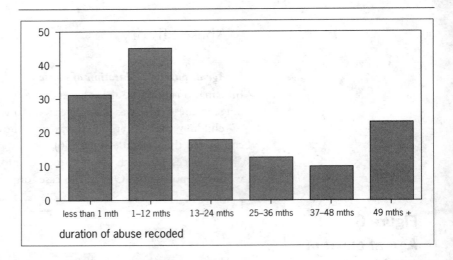

duration of abuse recoded

Among cases for whom we had information, duration did not vary with the gender of the victim, not with the relationship with the abuser.

Type of abuse experienced

Information about the abuse experiences of the children came from a variety of sources. Sometimes there were detailed reports from the police interview, or from case conferences, but this was a minority of cases. The most usual record was from the allocated family social worker.

Social workers were asked to record under sixteen headings the type of abuse experienced by the child. Information was available for 163 sexually abused children and teenagers, for whom 412 'types' of experience were reported. The full range of 'types' is given in Appendix 2, but in the main analysis these were condensed into three groups: non-contact, contact but non-penetrative, and penetrative (also shown in Appendix 2). The proportions in each of these categories are shown in Figure 8.

Figure 8
Types of abuse experienced by victims

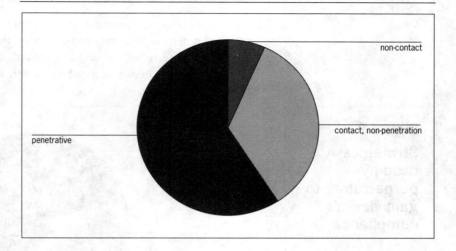

Overall 7% of the children had experienced non-contact abuse, 33% contact but non-penetrative abuse, and 60% had penetrative experiences. In the latter two groups many children experienced 'lesser' forms of abuse before their most serious experiences. There is strong evidence of the escalation of demands by the perpetrator, affecting the majority of children. Of the 163 children reporting some classifiable information, 108 (66%) reported two types of experience, 70 (43%) reported three types, 40 (25%) reported four types, 31 (19%) reported five types, and 21 (13%) reported six types.

The proportion experiencing penetrative abuse increased when children reported more types of abuse, indicating that many of them had experienced an escalation of demands from non-contact, through non-penetrative to penetrative abuse.

The closer the relationship (in a social sense) between the victim and the abuser, the more likely it was that penetrative abuse had occurred. For the 161 cases for whom we had information, penetrative abuse had occurred with 64% of fathers,[6] 25% of other family, and 11% of non family (x^2=10.31, 2df, p <.01).

The perpetrator's strategies to ensure compliance and to prevent the victim from disclosing

Information was available for 138 cases on the strategies used by the perpetrator both to ensure the child's compliance with the intended abuse, and their subsequent silence over what had happened.[7] The responses were rated under several headings which were re-coded into three main groups:

---

[6] 'fathers' includes surrogate fathers and three mothers
[7] Information was collected separately for compliance and preventing disclosure. There was a high level of agreement between these two, and only one measure is given here.

the use of bribery, deception or the simple 'authority' of an older/stronger person; non-violent threats (to the victim, the family or others); and the use of violent threats (to the child or others) or actual violence. The 'worst' experience of manipulation or violence that the child experienced is given below (Figure 9).

**Figure 9
Strategies used by perpetrators to gain victim's compliance**

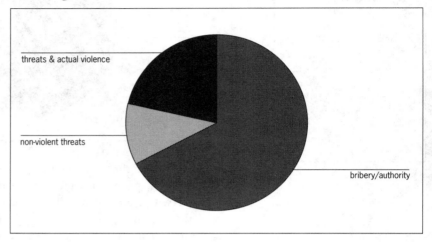

It did appear that referral agencies and centre staff put no particular value on obtaining this information, and, in support of this view, there is some evidence that this may not distinguish much between victims' psychological status at referral. However, it is clear that it would remain an important part of the victims' experiences with implications for clinical work. For example, among those for whom we had information there was no association between these strategies and levels of fear, self-esteem or depression at referral. There was also no association with age, or with relationship to the perpetrator. There was, however, a significant association with the type of abuse experienced: 10% of non-contact cases, 23% of contact cases and 51% of penetrative cases experienced violence and threats of violence (x^2=14.56, 4df, p <.01). It thus appears that those who experience the most severe forms of abuse, also stand the greatest chance of being a victim of violent behaviour by the perpetrator. Even so, about half of the children with experience of penetration have *not* met with violent behaviour as well. With hindsight, the association between these different aspects of violence might appear obvious, but we believe this information adds an important dimension to the context of the total abuse experience and should therefore routinely be asked about.

In addition, we should draw attention to the fact that these strategies may form part of the wider scheme for manipulating and grooming the victim. We believe that more attention should be given to the short- and long-term effects of such manipulation. For example, while the experience of aggression or violence may lead to some persisting and not unreasonable fears which may be highly protective in later settings, some forms of grooming experience will make a child more, rather than less, vulnerable. This will be particularly the case if the grooming has taken place over long periods of time or been generalized into other areas of interaction within the relationship.

Disclosure and discovery

Despite the pressure put on children not to disclose, many do so. How they choose to do this is important. For those cases for whom we had information we found that children were more likely to disclose to parents (72/166), and predominantly to mothers (68/72), than to any other group. Table 3 shows the people to whom the child disclosed or who made the discovery by their gender. Since mothers' reactions to the abuse discovery has been found to have an association with her child's coping capacities (see below), it is important to be aware how many mothers are involved at such early stages in the process of uncovering the abuse and taking the first steps to resolving the difficulties. This argues for support to be provided at the earliest stages of investigation to the mothers who have already carried such a high degree of their children's trust. Professionals to whom children disclosed included those involved in the early investigation after expression of concern by others. Five children did not disclose at any stage, and the evidence for their abuse experience came from other sources.

Table 3 **The people to whom the children disclosed**

Role	Female	Male
Mother/father	68	4
Sister/brother	4	2
Other relations	10	12
Adult friend	7	4
Child friend	9	3
Professional	29	14

The reactions of the primary carer to disclosure

Several studies have noted the important part in the child's recovery from trauma that family support plays. For example, Goodman et al (1992) and Everson et al (1991) noted that maternal support led to more rapid recovery of the child. In the child sexual abuse literature the early phase of such support is frequently represented by parental belief in the child's story.

In the current study, the very large majority of primary carers/mothers (138/161—86%) were reported as fully believing the child's story about the abuse by the time they had reached the stage of being referred for therapy. A further 11 mothers (7%) believed part of the story, but 12 mothers (8%) rejected the story entirely. However, mothers' levels of belief were not associated with the children's self-esteem scores or CDI scores at the time of referral. This was probably an artifact arising from the fact that such a high proportion of the mothers (and other primary carers) were reported as believing the children that it ceased to be a discriminating measure. It was clear that several therapists did not investigate the issue of maternal belief or support.

It might therefore be useful to consider other aspects of the reaction of parents as well as belief in the victim's story. For example, it may be important to distinguish those parents (mothers) whose belief in the story empowers them to act protectively and those whose belief leads to disabling helplessness and an inability to find solutions.

The Behaviour and Symptoms of the Victims

The Children's Depression Inventory (CDI)

Of 197 children over 8 years, 185 (94%) completed the CDI at the time of referral. Scores ranged from 0 to 43, with a mean of 15.87 (SD: 8.7). Two-thirds of the children (122—66%) scored over the standardised cut-off point of 18/19, which is a significantly higher proportion than would be expected from a similarly-aged normal population. These high levels of depressive symptoms have been noted in other studies of sexually abused children. For example, Koverola, Pound, Heger & Lytle (1993) found that 67% of a small sample of girls aged 6–12 years could be classified as experiencing depressive symptoms consistent with a diagnosis of depression. Kendall-Tackett et al. (1993) note that depression is a particularly 'robust' symptom across all age-groups, even though it has also been noted that girl victims tend to under-report their own depression compared with adults reports on them (Cohen & Mannarino, 1988).

In the present study there were no differences in CDI scores at referral between girls and boys.

The total CDI score was not associated with the relationship between perpetrator and victim, or with duration of abuse, but it was associated with the experience of penetrative abuse (compared with non-contact or contact/non-penetrative abuse) (one-way analysis of variance: $F=3.36$, 2df, $p <.04$). Koverola et al. (1993) found no association of depression with severity of abuse, but other studies have reported a significant association. However, it must be noted that 'severity of abuse' is recorded in different ways in different studies: we have chosen to keep the components separate and tested each component against the CDI scores. Other studies have reported 'severity' as one factor.

The CDI items on which more than 15% of the children checked the most severe category are given in Table 4. It will be noted that when the moderate and severe symptoms counts are combined these eight items were all checked by more than half the children. The high percentage recording *suicidal ideation* has implications for the type of support offered to these children, and is particularly interesting in view of the opinion expressed by some social workers that this question should not be asked. However, with one exception, there was no obvious pattern to the occurrence of suicidal ideation in the children: for example, suicidal ideas were not associated with having experienced penetrative abuse, or with the main abuser having been the father. Clearly there should be further studies of what components of the abuse experience are most likely to lead to suicidal thoughts or behaviour.

However, *suicidal ideation* was significantly more likely in those over 13 years (t–value-3.32, 163 df, p <.001). In other studies investigating suicidal ideation among sexually abused young people, adolescents have been found to be more at risk than younger age-groups (Kendall-Tackett et al., 1993). However, there is a sharp rise in successful suicide and attempted suicide after puberty in the population at large (Shaffer & Piacentini, 1994). Kendall-Tackett et al. (1993) note that out of seven studies which investigated suicidal ideation only one study found a difference in this symptom between sexually abused children and normal controls. Most suicidal ideas occur in the context of generalized depressive feelings (Shaffer & Piacentini, 1994), but only about one quarter of those expressing such ideas have a diagnosis of depression (Taylor & Stansfield, 1984). Other psychiatric diagnoses are also found such as conduct disorder (Kingsbury, 1993), emphasising the importance of assessing the full range of symptoms the young person may be showing. Asking about suicidal ideation can be appropriately undertaken when attendance at a specialist clinic ensures appropriate protective support.

Table 4 **Items on the Children's Depression Inventory on which the most severe score (2) was checked by more than 15% of the victims**

Item	Symptom score	
	0, 1 N (%)	2 N (%)
Loneliness	72 (37)	31 (16)
No fun at school	70 (37)	31 (16)
Not as good as others	71 (37)	33 (17)
Problems with school work	54 (28)	35 (18)
Eating problems	42 (22)	37 (19)
Sleep problems	50 (26)	44 (23)
Aches & pains	79 (41)	45 (23)
Suicidal ideation	56 (31)	45 (23)

It is perhaps noteworthy that three of the high-score items from the CDI are school-based; this raises the issue of whether better support should not be organised in school for abused children. We will return to this point in the section on Identification of Needs (below).

Victims' self-esteem scores

The self-esteem questionnaire was completed by 187 children (95% of those eligible). Scores varied between 19 and 132 (mean of 88.6; SD 22.8).

Self-esteem scores were significantly higher for boys than girls (t-test, $t=2.31$, 201 df, p <.001). As we have already noted, total self-esteem scores were inversely and significantly related to CDI scores: that is to say, the more depressed the victim was, the lower their self-esteem (Pearson's $r=-.614$, 199 cases, p <.001). There was a non-significant tendency for total self-esteem scores to be lower when the abuser was a father or father surrogate.

The scores for the domains of self-esteem are given in Table 5. The importance to the victims of their relationship with their mothers is emphasised by the relative scores: whether the responses in relation to mothers represents an idealised range or some version of 'reality' does not diminish the central role mothers occupy in their children's perceptions of themselves. The low position of 'school' scores again suggests the importance of working more closely with teachers to (re-)establish the victim's status in the school setting.

Table 5 **Victims' scores in domains of self-esteem**

Domain	Max Score	Mean Score	SD
Global self-esteem	(30)	20.3	6.3
In relation to mother	(15)	12.1	3.2
In relation to family	(15)	10.3	3.2
In relation to peers	(15)	9.4	3.3
In relation to father	(15)	9.3	4.4
Body image	(15)	9.0	3.9
In relation to school	(15)	8.9	3.5

The Fears Schedule

Among the 190 children aged 8 years and over who completed the 48-item shortened FSSC-R, scores ranged from 55 to 132 (mean: 92.7; SD: 16.0). These scores were not significantly different from the scores obtained at the development stage of the shortened questionnaire with a normal sample of 8–18 year olds. There were significant gender differences: girls recording higher scores than boys (t-value=3.72, 181 df, p <.001), but no age differences. [This gender difference persisted into Time 2 scores.]

As we have noted above (Measures), interpreting scores on individual items is not a useful exercise. However, it may be worth noting that the fears which were checked by more than 40% of the children are not substantially different from those recorded by the sample on which the shortened version was originally tested, although in both cases they are different from those reported by Ollendick et al. (1991) (Table 6). One striking feature of this abused sample is the extent of the fears around dying and death and about the fear of being separated from parents.

Table 6 **Individual items on the Fears Schedule for which at least 40% of the children expressed 'a lot of fear'**

Item	% scoring 'a lot of fear'
Mother dying	75
Being kidnapped	70
Not being able to breathe	61
Dying	57
Separation from parents	52
Burglars	52
Father dying	51
Being adopted	51
Falling from height	50
Meeting strangers	50
Getting lost in a strange place	49
Death or dead people	45
Nightmares	42
Choking	40

The Child Behavior Checklist (CBCL)

The CBCL was completed by parents (almost all mothers) some additional carers, teachers and the young people over 11 years. The results are given in Table 7 below.

Only 91 teachers' CBCLs were available on the children as they entered treatment. A number of factors contributed to the low response from teachers: obviously, some of the younger children were not in school. But, in addition, parental or youth permission to approach the school was withheld in some cases, some teachers said they were unable to help, and some centres decided that it was not helpful for schools to know that the children were attending the Centre. In two centres, staff were very concerned that the local schools had been infiltrated by paedophile rings, and that asking for information would mean that the child would subsequently be targeted by the ring members. In a handful of schools teachers reported that they did not have time to complete the Checklist.

Table 7 **Results of the Child Behavior Checklist from mothers, teachers and sexually abused children**

Informant	(N)	Mean Score	Range	SD
Mothers and other carers				
Total Problems	(163)	66.19	26–88	10.68
Internalizing Problems	(163)	61.42	33–88	10.64
Externalizing Problems	(163)	63.89	37–84	9.69
Teachers				
Total Problems	(91)	59.76	32–85	10.96
Internalizing Problems	(91)	57.95	36–93	12.44
Externalizing Problems	(91)	57.46	39–84	10.57
Abused children				
Total Problems	(110)	62.5	37–97	11.24
Internalizing Problems	(110)	62.1	35–96	11.29
Externalizing Problems	(110)	59.23	30–91	11.66

Several of the young people rated themselves as having problems which put them in the 'clinical' or 'borderline' range of scores (Table 8). Of the three raters, it appears that the mothers/carers perceived the largest numbers of symptoms in the children. One obvious explanation might have been that mothers/carers were accurately rating worse behaviour in children who were too young themselves to complete the Youth Self-Report. However, this was not the case: neither mothers nor teachers rated children under 11 years as showing more severe symptoms.

Agreement between mothers/carers and teachers could only be checked for 69 cases, but among these, agreement was statistically significant (although not very high) for all three scores (Pearson's two-tailed test: Total Problem scores: 0.368, p <003; Internalizing Problems: 0.386, p <.001; Externalizing Problems: 0.257, p <.04).

Agreement between the victims and their mothers/carers reached slightly higher levels, and were also significant (Total Problems: 0.506, p <001; Internalizing Problems: 0.464, p <.001; Externalizing Problems: 0.509, p <.001). Agreement between teachers and children only reached significance for the Total Problems (Pearson's two-tailed test: 0.467, p <.01).

Mothers/carers scored the children as showing higher Total Problem scores and Internalizing Problems and Externalizing Problems when the children had high CDI scores (Total problems: t-value=4.46, 2-tail p <0.001; Internalizing Problems: t-value=4.68, p <.001; and Externalizing Problems: t-value-3.83, 2-tail p <.001 respectively). Teachers also recorded significantly higher CBCL scores for the children with high CDI scores (Total Problems:

t-value=2.08, 2-tail p .041; and Internalizing Problems: t-value=2.26, 2-tail p .027). The children themselves recorded significantly higher Youth Self-Report scores when they also had higher CDI scores (Total Problems: t=value=5.77, 2-tail p=<.001; Internalizing Problems: t-value=5.74, 2-tail p=<.001; and Externalizing Problems: t-value=3.84, 2-tail p=<.001).

Table 8 **Child Behavior Checklist scores within the clinical or borderline ranges for three informants at the start of treatment: sexually abused children**

Informants	Clinical range	(%)	Borderline range	(%)
Mothers and other carers				
Total problems	67/163	(41)	10/163	(6)
Internalizing Problems	41/163	(25)	12/163	(7)
Externalizing Problems	50/163	(31)	19/163	(12)
Teachers				
Total Problems	17/91	(19)	11/91	(12)
Internalizing Problems	13/91	(14)	10/91	(11)
Externalizing Problems	14/91	(15)	3/91	(3)
Youth Self Report				
Total Problems	30/110	(27)	11/110	(10)
Internalizing Problems	22/110	(13)	16/110	(15)
Externalizing Problems	19/110	(17)	12/110	(11)

A check against the factors traditionally believed to determine 'severity' of abuse (duration, onset age, perpetrator being a parent and type of abuse) found that none were significantly associated with higher Child Behavior Checklist scores from any informant.

Sexualized behaviour

This is an area of behaviour which has frequently been cited as 'typical' of the sexually abused child. However, recent research has suggested that it is not found in more than a small proportion of confirmed cases (Monck et al. 1995; Kendall-Tackett et al, 1993), and the current findings support this view. Two questions were included in the current study, one of which was about whether the child was reported to be 'a sexual abuser' of other children. Social workers reported that 15 children (9%) showed this specific behaviour, while the very large majority (147—89%) did not (a response of 'not known' was given for 10 children).

When sexualized behaviour is reported in greater detail, only 79 out of 172 children are firmly described as showing no such behaviour at referral; (social workers did not know in a further 50 cases). The types of sexualized behaviour which had been observed among the remaining 43 children are given in Table 9; several children showed more than one type of sexualized behaviour.

Table 9 **Sexualized behaviour at referral (N=172)**

Reported behaviour	Frequency	
	(n)	**(%)**
None	79	(46)
Advances to other children	12	(7)
Advances towards adults	9	(5)
Uses age-inappropriate sexual words	9	(5)
Masturbates using objects	5	(3)
Masturbates with other children	3	(2)
Inserts objects into self/others	1	(–)
Sucks or licks others' genitalia	1	(–)
Initiates sexual intercourse	3	(2)
Not known	50	
Total	**172**	**(100)**

Identification of needs by therapists

We have provided a detailed description of the way in which these data were generated (Chapter 3). It is important to start with a caveat about the reliability of the information. Social workers provided reports which were doubly individualistic: each summary of needs referred to a particular child, but was also provided by someone working independently from the ratings given on other children by colleagues. Inevitably, this carries disadvantages.

Arising from the fact that the Identification of Needs was the final section in the data schedule which centre workers were asked to provide for each child, when the data schedule was missing so also was information on current needs. We thus have data on the current needs of only 172 children at Time 1.

As we noted earlier in this report, the Identification of Needs section was designed to maximise the opportunities for the therapeutic staff to record the full range of their concerns about the children and teenagers and their parents. Unfortunately, it became clear that some of the centre workers were asking the family's (community) social worker to complete the whole of the data schedule, including the section on the child's current needs, and the responses from these sources were less detailed than we had expected.

Clearly, the needs of the children and young people varied considerably as well, from gravely disturbed over a wide range of issues, to relatively well-adjusted and symptom-free.

The responses to this section were thus very variable. At one extreme detailed descriptions of current needs were given, suggesting an in–depth assessment and a detailed case history had been taken. At the other extreme, only a few words were recorded. When there were only a few items recorded it was difficult to tell if this was genuinely because the child had no needs (which raised issues around the entry into treatment), or because the person who filled in the Identification of Needs section did not feel able to give a fuller description, perhaps because they did not know the child and family well. It was also known that a small number of centre workers chose not to complete this section, even when they had the knowledge to do so.

Two examples of the entries are given below:

Example 1

This boy aged 6 years 2 months, was abused by his 11-year old brother, who, in turn, had been abused by a 17-year old male baby-sitter. The boy is now 'acting out sexually' with a neighbour's 'child' (NB. the gender of this latter child was not given).

Physical/medical needs: not known at this stage.

Psychological needs: not known at this stage, apart from helping W. to change his sexualized behaviour which will, in part, involve an understanding of his emotional needs.

Needs arising from discovery: an interruption of the repetitive features of abuse being passed on and abuse behaviour becoming generational.

Needs concerning sex education, etc: At this stage it would seem that sex education would benefit all members of the family.

Needs in relationships with family, peers, etc: specifically not known at this stage, but initially dyad work with his (abuser) brother would be anticipated and beneficial to both sibs.

Needs of family members: not known.

Needs of young person in school: not known.

Needs of mother/primary carer: Mother has been sexually abused by an uncle and a brother, and "speaks inappropriately about these". She appears to be limited in her current understanding of what she should do for her children who have been abused.

Strengths: W. appears to be a lively, bright and engaging child. He seems happy to have attended for his initial meeting.

Below we give a number of other verbatim examples of entries, the variability of which speaks for itself.

Examples

Psychological needs: D. needs to be able to accept correction, criticism, instructions and sanctions without immediately, or preemptively, assuming 'global' rejection or dislike. He needs to accept that he need only take responsibility for his own safety & protection as is age-appropriate (e.g., when with his biological parents he effectively protected himself from them by staying out late or running away—he dreaded coming back; now he must accept being in when his foster parents decide. [v010]

Needs of mother: J's mother is in the initial stages of dealing with her own abuse history. This needs to continue to enble her to support J., and to increase her own self-confidence. She has identified that her feelings about men have influenced her relationship with her son (the abuser of her daughter). [v095]

Strengths: N. has coped amazingly well considering what she has had to deal with. There are many positive things in her life, and she has strength of character and hopefully will get past the current difficulties now she feels free to express her feelings. [v006]

J is an extremely strong, resilient character who engaged very easily. I feel confident that she identifies risk areas now and is growing an awareness of her own wishes within future sexual relationships. She knows she is supported and loved by her mother. [v095]

At times the notes on 'needs' were difficult to interpret (e.g., *'Feelings around disclosure need to be explored and dealt with.'*; needs re sex education: *'All aspects.'*; Mother's needs: *'Mother needs supportive counselling.'*) It is important to record two reasons for commenting on the lack of detail. First, where the notes were very brief or very general it was difficult to rate the individual 'needs'.

Second, the absence of such detail sharply reduced the chances of recording how much change had taken place by the end of treatment or the end of the year. We recognise that the identification of needs in most cases takes place during the therapeutic intervention, and we agreed that centre workers might like to complete the schedules over several weeks. Many took advantage of this to provide very full descriptions of 'needs' as they became apparent. But, it is clear that therapists started their work at very different stages in the overall identification of needs.

The proportions of children with needs identified at Time 1 are shown in Table 10. Numbers were small or non–existent in relation to court proceedings.

Set against this picture of a high level of needs over a wide spectrum, centre workers identified that 25% of the children had positive attributes of their own, or strengths in their family or local networks which would act to protect them in future, and to improve their chances of surviving the current abuse situation. Unfortunately, it was clear that on this item (as no doubt on others) the individual perspective of the centre worker was crucially important: certain workers took a more optimistic approach and quite obviously sought out the positive attributes in the child and her environment. This must throw doubt on whether only a quarter of the children had these advantages, or whether this figure is a reflection of reporting bias.

Only one area of 'need' was related to gender of the child, and that was relationships with peers, in which the boys were significantly more likely to be recorded as showing difficulties.

Table 10 **Percentage of children with some identified needs in problem area**

Problem area	Percentage of children with some identified needs in problem area
Sex education needs	66%
Self-image problems	65%
Psychological problems	59%
Problems of personal safety	48%
School problems	37%
Arising from sexual abuse	35%
Conduct problems	32%
Post-traumatic stress symptoms	33%
Problems with peers	22%
Physical ill-health/disabilities	17%
Need to see other psychiatry or psychology professionals	4%

A total needs score was derived from a sum of the individual scores (not including the item on strengths). At the start of treatment scores ranged from 0 (only seven children) to 11 (mean 5.3; SD 2.3). Where one might have expected that (all other things being equal) the total needs score would be related to the type of abuse experience this was not found to be the case.

The Impact on Mothers

Questionnaire responses

The General Health Questionnaire was completed by 152 mothers: scores ranged from 36 to 35 (mean: 8.29; SD: 8.0), and more than half the women (55%) scored over the cut-off point indicating a risk of depressive or anxious disorders. The mothers of girls reported significantly higher GHQ scores than the mothers of boys. The mean scores on the sub-categories of the GHQ were as follows: anxiety—9.4 (SD 5.9); social dysfunction—8.2 (SD 3.3); somatic symptoms—6.8 (SD 4.4); and depression—4.6 (SD 5.9). The most frequent cluster of symptoms was around anxiety and social dysfunction, rather than depressive mood.

The *Beck Depression Inventory* was completed by only 145 mothers (61%). Scores ranged from 0 to 47, with a mean of 15.03 (SD: 11.78). A large proportion of these mothers (42%) scored over the established cut-off point, suggesting the possibility of depressive illness, although only a clinical interview could establish this. Wagner (1991) noted that BDI scores of mothers of sexually abused children did not differ significantly from the scores of mothers of non-abused children. However, there was a tendency for mothers of children abused by perpetrators outside the family to record higher scores.

At referral, higher scores on the mothers' GHQ and the BDI were associated with their child scoring above the cut-off point on the CDI (t-test: t=2.43, 67df, p <.02; and t=2.11, 65df, p <.04, respectively).

Adult self-esteem inventory. Only 144 mothers completed the self-esteem inventory. Their scores ranged from 35 to 131. On this inventory there is no cut-off point defining respondents as having 'high' or 'low' self-esteem, but it is striking that the women with high self-esteem were producing scores four times those of the women at the lower end of the scale. Mothers' recorded higher scores in the domains of 'Self as someone who cares for others' (mean 10.0; SD 1.6), 'Moral self' (mean 8.5; SD 1.9) and 'Self as provider for household' (mean 8.3; SD 2.4); and lowest on 'having and being a confidant (mean 7.0; SD 2.3) and body image (mean 6.2; SD 2.8).

In a repetition of the finding about the child's gender and maternal depressive mood, the self-esteem of the mothers was significantly associated with the gender of the victim: mothers of girls showing lower self-esteem scores.

Clinically identified needs of mothers

Information on a narrower range of issues was reported for parents, and recorded under two headings: the parents' own needs and parenting problems. Table 11 gives the proportions of parents who were identified as having problems in these areas, and the level of identified needs among siblings.

Table 11 **Identification of parents' problems at the time of referral (N=167)**

Problem area	Percentage of parents and siblings with identified needs in problem area
Parents' own needs	62%
Parenting problems	54%
Siblings needs	14%

Part 2

The Young Perpetrators

Availability of Information from Questionnaires and Schedules

Information was available from schedules completed by centre workers for only 39 out of the 55 boys at Time 1 (71%), 19 boys at Time 2 and only 10 boys at Time 3. The latter all attended the same treatment centre in Northern Ireland. The responses from each set of informants is set out in Figure 10.

**Figure 10
Data Protocols received from centres**

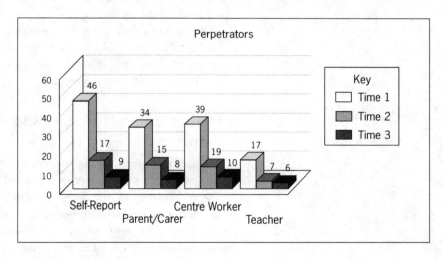

It is, by definition, not possible to say if the boys on whom no information was supplied differed in significant ways from those for whom we had information. However, boys sometimes completed self-report questionnaires even when the centre workers had given no background information. From this it was clear that the boys whose social workers had not supplied information did not differ in their scores on the Children's Depression Inventory or the Self-esteem Inventory from those whose social worker had provided information.

Of the 55 boys who could have filled in the self-report questionnaires, 46 did so at Time 1, 17 at Time 2, and 9 at Time 3. The fall-off at Times 2 and 3 arose partly because some boys had not completed their treatment programmes when the research ended, while for others there was a straightforward failure to get the questionnaires filled in.

Among mothers, 34 filled in the questionnaires (both self-report and reports on their sons) at Time 1, 15 at Time 2 and eight at Time 3. Again, the reasons why mothers did not complete all the questionnaires was complex: sometimes there was no parental figure, in which case only the parents' version of the Child Behavior Checklist was filled in by other carers. At Time 1, two foster parents and four care workers completed the CBCL on the boys. At Time 2 some boys had not finished their treatment; and in relation to Time 3 questionnaires, some boys had not reached the one-year point; in such circumstances the parents (and surrogate parents) would not have been approached for more information.

As a separate but important point, it is worth recording that only three centres accepted ten or more boys into their programmes during the lifetime of the research. One centre accepted eight boys, and two had four boys each, but five centres only saw one young perpetrator. This raises the issue of whether it is always appropriate or cost effective to develop a body of expertise within a team in this specialist field if it is only going to be used once a year. Clearly this is a policy issue on which it would be wrong for researchers to comment. From the research point of view, however, it greatly increases the difficulty of interpreting results.

Demographic Characteristics of the Young Perpetrators

All the young perpetrators in this sample were boys. This is currently not unusual when a specialist service is offered (Will, 1995).

Twenty of the boys attended centres in Northern Ireland, and the rest had been referred to centres in England. The majority (45) were not subject to any legal orders; seven boys were on probation, one boy (in N. Ireland) was attending Training School. Only one boy was recorded as being of mixed race, 38 were white European, while information is missing for the remaining 16. It is particularly unfortunate that this information is missing for such a large proportion of the sample, as there is considerable current debate around providing suitable programmes for youngsters from ethnic minorities. The planning of such services must suffer if appropriate records are not kept.

Ages at referral ranged from 10 years to 19 years 6 months (mean: 14.96). The young perpetrators tended to come from large families (range 1–7 children; mean 3.6), but this was probably a product of the large number from Northern Ireland centres. Only one boy was an only child. Nevertheless, the number of siblings 'at risk' is of particular interest in view of the number of sibling-victims (see below).

At the time of abuse, most boys for whom we had information were living with two parental figures: 16 (41%) with their own parents, 12 (31%) with their mother and her partner, and one (3%) with his father and partner. Five boys (13%) lived with mother alone, two with father alone, two were in institutions, and one was in fostercare. Nearly two-thirds of mothers were married, and only 5% were single. These figures should not be taken as representative of young perpetrators across the United Kingdom as divorce is less common in N. Ireland, where a significant number of the boys lived. At the time of referral these figures had hardly changed at all, in contrast to the family circumstances of the abused children nearly half of whom landed up living with mothers alone.

One father was known to have a previous conviction for sexual assault against children, and one mother had a conviction for a non-violent crime. It may be noted that this group of fathers (including current mothers' partners) appears to have a lower level of previous criminal convictions than the 'fathers' of the abused children, but figures were not checked with police or Home Office records, and were anyway not available for the parents of 16 boys.

The Background and Childhood of the Young Perpetrators

In half the 21 boys for whom centre workers provided information there was a history of earlier sexual victimisation (11/21–52%). This was very similar to the proportions found in other studies, reviewed by Watkins & Bentovim (1992) and reported by Will (1995). There was also commonly a history of physical abuse when information was available: 13 out of 25 boys were reported as having been physically abused in childhood, five out of 20 boys had been neglected, and 9 out of 18 had been emotionally abused.

As we have seen the family backgrounds appear relatively stable, compared to those of the abused children, but despite this several of the boys (n=16: 41%) had spent long periods in their childhood away from their biological parents. Three boys had never lived with their own parents, and another eleven had spent periods of as little as one year with theirs. Six boys had been fostered for periods of between one and four years, although only one was still fostered at the time of referral. Fourteen boys (including six who had been fostered) had, at times, been in institutional care: ten of them in only one institution, but four of them had been placed in more than two Homes, and two were in Children's Homes at the time of referral. Other research studies also report high levels of disrupted family life. For example, data on over 1,000 adolescent offenders found 57% had experienced parental loss, and only 28% were living with both parents at the time of their offenses (National Adolescent Perpetrator Network, 1988).

Education and work histories

At the time of referral five young men had already left school. Two had work and one was unemployed (no information on two). Of the remainder, 25 (74%) were in mainstream schools and nine (27%) were in special schools. Eleven young perpetrators (33% of those on whom we had information) had Statements of Special Educational Needs, which was significantly more than might be expected of a non-psychiatric adolescent male population. It was not clear if the Statements had been prepared as a result of issues around sexually abusive behaviour, or whether they arose from other concerns by teachers or parents. Several previous studies have suggested the difficulties young perpetrators experience at school, sometimes from disturbed behaviour (e.g., Kahn & Chambers, 1991), and sometimes from low achievement (e.g., Saunders & Awad, 1988; Beckett et al, in press).

Referrals, preliminary investigation

Information was available for 36 cases only. Of these the majority (29—74%) were referred by social services, one from a General Practitioner, two (5%) from the courts, and seven (18%) from probation.

Previous history of abusive behaviour

Unfortunately, information on the background of the young perpetrators was also missing for many. Thirty-three were described as having no previous convictions, and three had a previous criminal record for sexual (1) and non-sexual (2) crimes. Seventeen young perpetrators (46%) had already received some therapeutic intervention for the abusive behaviour, the largest single group (7) being treated by social services.

Characteristics of the Abusive Acts

The age at first committing a sexual offence ranged from 9–18 years (mean: 13.9) and in most cases referred to the start of the current event or series of sexual offenses which brought the young man into treatment.

Gender and number of victims Of the 36 perpetrators for whom information was available, 28 (78%) had abused between them 51 females (mean: 1.8), and 14 (39%) had abused between them 30 males (mean: 2.1). Thirty perpetrators (83%) abused only one gender, while six (17%) abused children of both genders; this is considerably lower than the 30% found abusing both genders by Kahn & Lafond (1988). Twenty-three boys (64%) admitted to offenses against at least two victims, eleven against at least three victims, and 7 against four or more victims.

Age differences between victim and perpetrator Data on the age difference between the young perpetrator and his victims showed that there was a considerable range, but the mean age of the victims was substantially below the mean age of the perpetrators. For the first victims mean difference in age was 6.1 years, for the second victims the mean difference was 5.3 years, for the third 8.3 years, and for the fourth 6.2 years; three young perpetrators had sexually attacked older women. Among the 65 victims for whom there was information, 30 (46%) were less than five years younger than the perpetrator, and of these 10 (15%) were less than two years younger.

Relationship between victim and perpetrator Where the relationship between the perpetrator and his victims was known, the commonest two categories were siblings (25/77–32%), and 'other', covering children attending the same school who were not friends, and 18 (23%) who were the children of neighbours. There is almost certainly an element of opportunism in the younger perpetrator's sexual assaults, which is why the family group and the neighbour's children form such a large proportion overall. The evidence from US studies of adolescent abusers suggests that easy access to the victim is important. Kahn & Lafond (1988) found 95% of abusers knew their victim; Kahn & Chambers (1991) found one third of victims were known but lived in another household, while 28% were siblings. Nevertheless, the point has been made to us by experienced workers, that even where victims are known or related to the perpetrator, they are the target of 'grooming' beforehand in many cases.

The proximity of the victim must have some bearing on placement and other legal decisions about the perpetrator. As Hughes & Parker (1994) have pointed out, it is not in the interests of children generally that such high proportion of sexual abuse perpetrators are still able to move freely in the community 'as an unchecked risk', and this is as true for the young as the for adult perpetrator.

Most of the young perpetrators acted alone (28/39–72%) and in no instance was any boy involved in an organised ring, and in no case was there any evidence of ritualistic abuse.

It can thus be seen that the common pattern is for the young perpetrator to abuse more than one victim, more often than not of one gender, nearly all substantially younger than himself. However, it is important to note that the age difference between victims and perpetrators was, in a substantial minority of cases, less than five years. These figures tend to confirm the picture suggested in other descriptive studies of adolescent perpetrators and reports of adults sex offenders describing their own teenage activities.

Context and Types of abusive acts

Any idea that younger perpetrators engage on relatively minor forms of sexual abuse is dispelled by nearly all studies (Wasserman & Kappel, 1985; Will, 1995). In the current study the abusive actions ranged from rape to exhibitionism. In each case it was possible to record up to six different abusive actions: thus one boy had initially fondled his sister's genital area, progressed to genital-to-genital contact, digital vaginal penetration, getting his sister to masturbate him and finally attempting vaginal intercourse. The categories are listed in Appendix D.

A total of 88 separate activities were reported, of which the single most common category was fondling the victim inappropriately (18/88–20%). The activities were rated in three categories: non-contact, contact but non-penetrative, and penetrative. The largest group is those activities which involved contact but were not penetrative (53–60%), while non-contact activities and penetration both formed 20% of reported experiences (Figure 11). Age at referral of the young perpetrator was not related to the severity of these activities. It is thus clear that even at relatively young ages these boys might be involved in the full range of sexual abusive actions.

**Figure 11
Types of
Sexually
Abusive
Activity**

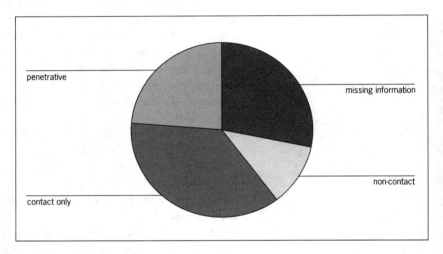

The legal offenses

Several of the boys were or had been subject to legal procedures which meant that their sexual offenses had been classified. The figures are given in Table 12. For 26 boys there was no court case, and in three cases which came to court the boys pleaded guilty.

Actions taken by young perpetrator to gain victim's compliance and ensure victim did not tell anyone about the abuse

Information was available on these two points for a minority of the young perpetrators (25 only). These boys reportedly used 31 strategies to ensure compliance: 20 (65%) used only bribery, deception or the 'authority' of being older (which can be very threatening); five used non-violent threats (e.g. of

Table 12 **Current offenses**

Type of offense	N
Gross indecency	3
Buggery	1
Indecent assault	16
Unlawful intercourse with girl over 13 years	2
girl under 13 years	2
Incest	2
Exhibitionism	4
Other	2
No charge	2
Not reported by Centre workers	21

change to the household), and six used threats of, and actual violence against the victim. This latter group included, for example, a boy who tried to rape a girl in the school playground while his friend held her down; although he was not successful, the girl was bruised and very frightened, especially when the boy said next time he would succeed because he would have two friends with him. It is particularly unfortunate that we have such an incomplete picture of the actions taken by the boys during the assaults, which would contribute usefully to any prediction of risk and to an understanding of the strategies used by younger perpetrators.

The same categories were used to classify the actions taken by the young perpetrators to prevent the victims telling other people. The 25 boys for whom there is information used 30 strategies for ensuring silence of the victim (i.e. some used more than one device): 21 (70%) used bribery, deception or 'authority'; three used non-violent threats, and six used violent threats. Rubenstein et al. (1993) investigated the adult outcome of young sexual perpetrators who used violence in their assault. Compared with violent non-sexual young offenders, the sexual offenders were significantly more likely to commit violent non-sexual, as well as sexual, offenses in adulthood. Such studies suggest the importance of establishing more clearly than was always the case in the present study, the strategies used by young perpetrators to carry out their assaults and silence the victims.

Psychological Status of Young Perpetrators at Referral

It will be recalled that the young perpetrators were given a booklet of questionnaires for self-completion. The following section describes the information derived from these self-report questionnaires.

Children's Depression Inventory

Forty-six boys completed the CDI; scores ranged from 1 to 29, with a mean of 10.8 (SD 7.2). Only 15% of the boys scored over the established cut-off point indicating the risk of depressive disorder. This is not significantly greater than the 10% which could be expected from a non-clinic, community sample of boys in the same age-group.

Individual items were seldom given a high score: only four items were checked in the most pathological category by more than 10% of the boys. These items were 'thinking bad things will happen', 'having to push self to do school work', fatigue, and suicidal ideation.

The CDI scores were significantly and inversely related to self-esteem scores at referral. Those boys scoring above the cut-off point on the CDI had significantly lower self-esteem scores (t-test: t-value=4.77, 88.47, p <.0001).

None of the abuse variables which together compose severity of abusive behaviour (duration, relationship to victim and type of abuse) were associated with higher CDI scores.

Self-esteem inventory

Forty-one boys completed the Self-esteem Inventory at referral and scores ranged from 60–131 (mean 91.8; SD=16.72). Table 13 shows the mean scores for the subgroups on the self-esteem inventory.

The rank order of the domains of self-esteem is very similar to the rank order given by the victims (Table 5). Again, relationship with mother appears at the top of the list, but whether this is a realistic or an idealized picture of the importance to them of this relationship must be unclear. Again, school appears as the domain which provides the lowest score: an area of the young perpetrators' lives from which they draw least satisfaction.

Table 13 **Young perpetrators' scores on the Self-esteem inventory subgroups**

Subgroup	max. score	mean score
Global score	(30)	22.0
Relationship with mother	(12)	11.9
Body image	(12)	10.8
Place in the family	(12)	10.2
Relationship with peers	(12)	9.3
Relationship with father	(12)	9.0
School performance	(12)	8.9

Blame Attribution

Results from the Blame Attribution questionnaire will be presented in a separate paper.

The Child Behavior Checklist scores

At referral, 43 boys completed the Youth Self–Report, but fewer Checklists were available from mothers or teachers (Table 14.)

Table 14 **Child Behavior Checklist results for young perpetrators at referral**

Informant Checklist	(N)	Mean	Range	SD
Mother				
Total Problem Score	(31)	66.65	48–88	10.03
Internalizing Problems	(31)	61.13	45–80	9.42
Externalizing Problems	(31)	64.74	40–86	9.42
Teacher				
Total Problem Score	(16)	59.62	33–88	12.58
Internalizing Problems	(16)	58.38	38–69	9.75
Externalizing Problems	(16)	58.44	40–85	13.29
Youth				
Total Problem Score	(43)	55.33	35–84	11.08
Internalizing Problems	(43)	54.35	32–82	11.8
Externalizing Problems	(43)	55.74	43–84	9.63

On the teachers' CBCL scores, there was an association between age at referral and Externalizing teacher scores: the younger boys were rated by teachers as showing significantly higher Externalizing (acting-out) behaviour (t-value=2.23, 2-tail significance=<0.05). Age at referral was not associated with the boys' or mothers' scores.

Mothers with high General Health Questionnaire scores (5+) were significantly more likely to give their young perpetrator sons higher Total Problem and Internalizing Problem (but not Externalizing Problem) scores (Total Problems: t-value=2.22, 2-tail p=0.035; Internalizing Problems: t-value=2.80, 2-tail p=0.009). Among the boys themselves, higher Depression Inventory scores were significantly associated with higher Total Problem and Internalizing Problem scores (t-value=3.17, 2-tail p=0.003; and t-value=4.51, 2-tail p=<0.001 respectively).

Agreement was significant between mothers and teachers only on the Internalizing Problems (Pearson's corr: .668, p <.01), and agreement of the young perpetrators with either their mothers or their teachers were not significant.

The proportion of young perpetrators falling within the clinical range on the three versions of the Child Behavior Checklist varied with the informant. The figures are given in Table 15. Mothers were markedly more likely than the teachers to identify that their sons were highly symptomatic. The boys reported themselves as much less symptomatic than the (few) teachers or than their mothers did.

Table 15 **Child Behavior Checklist scores within the clinical or borderline ranges for the three informants at the start of treatment: young perpetrators**

Informant	clinical range	(%)	Borderline range	(%)
Mother				
Total Problem score	15/31	(48)	2/31	(6)
Internalizing Problems	5/31	(16)	5/31	(16)
Externalizing Problems	12/31	(39)	3/31	(9)
Teacher				
Total Problem score	3/16	(19)	1/16	(6)
Internalizing Problems	2/16	(13)	2/16	(13)
Externalizing Problems	3/16	(19)	1/16	(6)
Youth				
Total Problem score	4/43	(9)	1/43	(2)
Internalizing Problems	5/43	(12)	1/43	(2)
Externalizing Problems	4/43	(9)	—	—

Identification of needs

As with the victims, centre workers' reports on the outstanding needs of the young perpetrators varied considerably in the range and detail, as the following two examples show:

Example 3 (p 144)

Young male perpetrator, aged 13 yrs 6 mths, who had abused his sister over 8–10 incidents; abuse consisted of inappropriate touching and fondling, and making the girl touch his penis.

Physical/Medical needs: none apparent

Psychological needs: Needs to learn to control his urges to abuse. He needs to understand the impact of his behaviour

Needs arising from discovery: clear framework for work on S's offending.

Sexuality, etc: Work focused on relationships; valuing others.

Relationships with others: [no comment]

Other family members: work for victim. Work for mother.

School, etc: [no comment]

Other needs: [no comment]

Needs of mother/primary carers: She needs a framework in which to understand his behaviour. Needs to have the impact of her son's behaviour on her acknowledged.

Strengths, etc: [no comment]

Example 4

Young male perpetrator, aged 13 yrs 2 mths.

With a male peer holding the girl victim, S. attempted vaginal intercourse within the school grounds during the lunchbreak; he also fondled another girl inappropriately. It appeared there had only been two incidents.

Physical/medical needs: S. has suffered from migraines and is on medication. An EEG is planned to determine whether there is physiological reasons for his behaviour.

Psychological needs: S. presents as being emotionally very confused and disturbed. Such confusion/disturbance is conveyed through violent outbursts and verbal outbursts, particularly against adults, people in authority. He presents as having a love/hate perception of parents. He is very good and kind to younger children.

Needs arising from discovery: S. has difficulty in accepting responsibility re abuse; he appears to have 'lost control' re incident. Has very negative perception of females and is verbally very condemning of them.

Needs re sexuality etc: Does S. have personal/inner controls re what is acceptable/ unacceptable sexual behaviour?

Needs sex education: [none recorded]

Needs re others: S. has no respect re adults or authority figures unless he can dictate/ determine the agenda. S. wants to be leader in peer group situations.

Needs of family members: Mother has mental health problems; concerns re father's input into family life; youngest child (male) said by parents to be hyperactive: this view put strongly by mother.

Needs re school, etc.: S. is unable to accept guidance or advice from authority figures in school setting.

Other needs: Ongoing social work intervention re this family for several years in attempt to save the dysfunctional nature of the family.

Needs of primary carers: Mother has mental health problem, and has colluded in the past with S's unacceptable behaviour—tends to overreact to situations. Ongoing work with mother to address same; father has tended to take a non-active role in the past.

Strengths, etc: Social work staff and parents have commented that S. can be a very pleasant, cheerful and sensitive boy. On the other hand, residential social workers have noted bizarre behaviour, e.g. making himself sick, making strange noises, etc.

In order to illustrate that an informative style was not limited to individual entries, we have included some further examples drawn from a wide range of centres.

Examples

Psychological needs: 1. Very low self esteem, and socially isolated; peer relations not good; high level of anxiety; unresolved grief about Mom's death. [p121] 2. J. has violent outbursts at home and is subjected to his father's very strict moral & religious beliefs. Needs help to control anger, and get sense of normality. Is of low ability and lacks confidence. Needs to understand sexual norms and get sense of normality.

Needs in relationship of young person with family, etc: Very uncomfortable with peers; general social anxiety; sees self as different from peers; gravitates to younger children. [p121]

Strengths: C. is an intelligent 17 year old, who as a child witnessed his father abusing the immediate family. This may have precipitated his abuse of his sister, although C. does not excuse himself because of his background.

Table 16 shows the percentages of young perpetrators who were regarded as showing an outstanding 'need' in each area at the time of referral. As with the 'needs' recorded for the victims, it is not possible to distinguish those young perpetrators for whom there was no current 'need', from those where the centre worker chose not to rate a 'need', or where information was not available to the centre worker. The figures should therefore be approached with care.

Nevertheless, it is striking how small a proportion of these adolescents were recorded as having needs in areas which have been identified as crucially important in any therapeutic intervention with young perpetrators; for example, understanding their own cycle of abuse, building social skills, developing empathy or addressing cognitive distortions about children or women.

Table 16 **The outstanding needs identified for young perpetrators at the start of treatment (N=39)**

Young perpetrator's needs	%
1. to understand own cycle of abuse	51%
2. to manage emotions	44%
3. to build social skills	36%
4. to build self-esteem	33%
5. emotional security in family	21%
6. to develop empathy	21%
7. to control aggression	21%
8. to accept responsibility	18%
9. boundaries to behaviour	15%
10. to deal with cognitive distortions about children & women	13%
11. Sex Education issues	
a) learn age-appropriate behaviour	39%
b) general sex education	36%
c) control sexual behaviour	18%
d) non-coercive relationships	15%
e) learn appropriate touching	13%
f) future sexuality/choices	10%

Therapists were asked to identify any positive and supportive features of the young perpetrator or within his environment. In no case did therapists identify any support from families or from non-family, and in only two boys were temperamental strengths identified.

The Mothers of the Young Perpetrators

Questionnaire responses

General Health Questionnaire scores were available for 34 mothers: scores ranged from 0 to 27 [mean: 7.4; SD: 7.7], with two-thirds (66%) scoring over the cut-off point. Means for the four sub-scores were as follows: Anxiety—8.4 (SD: 6.2); social dysfunction—7.8 (SD: 2.1); somatic symptoms—6.5 (SD: 5.1); and depression—3.9 (SD: 4.9). The rank order of these sub-categories of the GHQ is the same as for the mothers of the victims.

The same 34 mothers completed the Beck Depression Inventory. The BDI is more specifically focussed on depressive symptoms than the GHQ, and 71% of these mothers did not score above the cut-off point. Half the mothers (53%) showed no depression, and 18% showed mild depressive symptoms.

As we have already noted, the mothers of the young perpetrators are sometimes the mothers of victims as well. We divided the mothers into three groups: mothers of victims, mothers of young perpetrators, and mothers of both victim and perpetrators. Although numbers were small and results must be approached with care, there were no differences between the three groups in their scores on self-report questionnaires on depression (GHQ & Beck), or self-esteem. There were also no differences in the level of identified parental needs between these three groups. We have not found references to the varied needs of parents who fall into these three groups and believe that this is an area in which further investigation should be undertaken.

Clinically identified needs of parents

The needs of parents[8] were broken down into two main groups: the need to strengthen parenting skills, and the parents' own needs.

Table 17 lists the proportions of parents who were identified with needs around parenting skills. It had been expected that the total parenting skills score would be associated with aspects of the young perpetrators' recorded 'needs'. However, parenting skills 'needs' were only associated with the presence of sex education 'needs' in the boys (x^2=4.67, 1df, p <.04). Total parenting skills 'needs' were not associated with the total 'needs' score of the

---

[8] In this context 'parents' refers to mothers or stepmothers; foster parents and Children's Home staff are excluded.

young perpetrators; in other words, the centre workers were not simply relating the parents' need to improve their skills to the size of the problem which faced them.

Table 17 **Parenting skill needs identified at the start of the young perpetrators' treatment**

Parent's needs	%
Help with understanding their boy's behaviour	25%
To give support to treatment	21%
Help coping with boy's behaviour	21%
Increase understanding of issues	21%
Enhancement of general skills	18%
To believe/support the boy	4%
To trust professionals	2%
To provide positive role model	2%

Table 18 lists the parents' own identified needs. This included issues such as on-going alcoholism or mental health needs, or the need to deal with the anger and distress of discovering their son was an abuser. The presence of parents' own 'needs' was significantly related to the self-reported Beck Depression Inventory scores, although not to parental self-esteem or GHQ scores. Two explanations are possible; it is possible that BDI scores are associated with the cluster of personal needs recorded here, or centre workers were particularly sensitive to the depressive symptomatology covered by the BDI, and this led to more careful consideration of parents' own needs.

Table 18 **Proportion of parents whose own needs were identified at the start of son's treatment**

Parental need	%
Own mental health, alcoholism, etc	16%
To deal with own victimisation	11%
Support for distress, guilt, etc	8%
To deal with anger with perpetrator	3%

Chapter 5

Some Comparisons Between the Victims and Young Perpetrators

It will be obvious that there were marked age and gender differences between the two groups of children and young people which make direct comparison difficult. Below we separately compare all young perpetrators with (a) the whole victim sample, (b) the male victims, and (c) the male victims over 10 years. The latter are the victims with whom comparison with the younger perpetrators is most appropriate.

Comparison of the Young Perpetrators with all Victims

On the standardised self-report measures, the victims showed significantly higher scores on the CDI (t-test: $t=3.65$, 229df, $p <.001$), but there were no differences on the single item of suicidal ideation. Total self-esteem scores of the victims and young perpetrators did not differ significantly at the time of their referral; on sub-scores the only observed difference was in body image (t-test: $t=3.28$, 83.1df, $p <.002$). The 144 mothers of victims who completed self-report measures, reported significantly higher scores on the Beck Depression Inventory than the 34 mothers of young perpetrators at Time 1 (t-test: $t=2.48$, 61.95df, $p <.02$). There were no significant differences between the mothers of young perpetrators and victims on their self-report scores on the General Health Questionnaire or its sub-scales, nor on the adult Self-esteem Inventory, and its sub-scores. The only group of identified needs to show a significant difference at Time 1, was the parents' own needs, where parents of victims were perceived as having more problems.

Comparison of Young Perpetrators with Male Victims

The childhood abuse and neglect of the young perpetrators and the male victims showed no significant differences, except that more male victims were thought to have experienced emotional abuse. However, most centre workers recording this information associated their rating of emotional abuse with the experience of sexual abuse, which may be true, but makes a comparison of abused boys and young perpetrators more difficult.

Here again the only trend towards a difference on the children and young people's self-report questionnaires was on the CDI scores, and this did not reach significance. Therapists rated the male victims as being significantly more likely to have needs around the issues of 'safety' (unresolved placement needs, parental protection from abuse, etc); this difference in reality reflected the fact that few of the young perpetrators had themselves been abused. There were no significant differences in identified needs in other area.

Comparison of the mothers of the young perpetrators and the male victims showed no differences in self-report scores. Therapists identified the victims' mothers as showing significantly more personal needs.

Comparison of Young Perpetrators with Male Victims aged 10 years or more

There were only 18 male victims aged 10 or more years, and again the only observed difference was a non-significant trend towards victims having higher CDI scores than young perpetrators. None of the other self-report scores discriminated between the two groups.

Comparison of the mothers of young perpetrators and male victims over the age of 10 years, showed that there was a tendency (which did not reach significance) for the mothers of the victims to have higher self-esteem and lower General Health Questionnaire scores t-tests: $t=2.07$, 16.88df, $p=.05$; and $t=1.96$, 23.76df, $p=.06$ respectively). The small numbers make interpretation of these findings uncertain.

Ethnicity of the Samples

Several centres with which we worked were located in cities which had relatively high proportions of their populations from minority ethnic communities, for example, Leeds, Leicester and Camberwell in S. London. Several teams of workers had undertaken special training in order to be able to provide appropriate help to sexually abused children and their families and young perpetrators from such minority groups. In the event only 7% of the sample came from these communities. While it was obviously right for the teams to prepare themselves to work with black and Asian families, clearly there needs to be further investigation of why few children from these families appeared in the treatment programmes. One possible explanation of the absence of young black perpetrators is because more are detained than young white perpetrators after a court case for sexual offending (Williams & Santry, submitted for publication). It is also possible that there are fewer young perpetrators in black and Asian families.

Summary

Surprisingly few differences were observed between the samples on standardised measures or levels of identified needs at Time 1. There is no obvious reason why this is so. However, therapists will certainly draw attention to the fact that although the self-reported score of a young perpetrator and a victim may be the same (for example, on individual CDI items or total scores) the *meaning* of those ratings may be profoundly different. This underlines the importance of not using standardised measures as a substitute for, but only a adjuncts to, sensitive enquiry on the full range of the individual child's or adolscent's needs.

Chapter 6

The Outcome of Treatment

Part 1

Outcomes for Victims and Their Mothers

The purpose of the project had been to provide detailed information about the progress of children through therapies. Unfortunately, for two main reasons information about the children at Time 2 (the end of treatment), and Time 3 (the end of the year) was limited. First, some children had not finished their treatment (and therefore had not reached Time 2). Additionally, some children had entered treatment less than 12 months from the end of the study, thus reducing the number eligible for Time 3 testing. Second, some centres did not provide the second tranche of information, or ask the children to fill in questionnaires even though they had finished treatment within the study timetable. A small number of children were reported as refusing to complete a second administration of questionnaires. The figures for available information have been given in Figure 2.

Attendance at the Treatment Centres

The most usual number of sessions chosen for treatment programmes was 10, or 12, but there was wide variation, from six to 35, with a mean of 12.6. The number of sessions actually attended by the victims was scarcely less—ranging from 3 to 36, with a mean of 11.3. This suggests that very few victims failed to attend for the full course.

The Effects of Therapeutic Intervention

Among the 66 victims for whom there was some information at Time 2 there were few significant changes over the period of the treatment. Symptoms, mood and behaviour were assessed using the standardised questionnaires and the clinically identified needs.

Questionnaire responses

Sixty children completed the Fears Schedule at Time 2 as well as Time 1. For these children there had been no significant change between the beginning and end of treatment. However, among the 42 children who completed the CDI and the Self-esteem Inventory, there had been significant improvement for the group as a whole over the treatment period. On self-esteem the scores of 27 children improved over the period, while the scores of 13 declined ($Z=-2.34$; 2-tailed $p <.02$). On the CDI, the scores of 30 children improved, and the scores of nine declined ($Z=-3.69$, 2-tailed $p <.0002$) [in each case the scores stayed the same for the remaining children].

Clinically Identified Needs

The small number of cases for whom needs had clearly been identified at referral made the chances of improvement quite limited. The majority of the 66 children for whom there was some information at time 2 from centre workers appeared to have identical levels of need at the start and end of treatment largely because no comment had been made at either time. Improvement was recorded by the centre workers on items around the children's self-esteem, and a reduction was recorded on items concerned with the need for sex education.

There were no other significant changes recorded by centre workers in the identified needs of the sexually abused children, but the 'strengths' identified for individual children showed a sharp improvement. Four children showed fewer strengths or positive factors in their environment, but greater strengths were observed for 23: there was no change for the rest.

Child Behavior Checklist (CBCL)

For the victims, Child Behavior Checklists were available from 55 mothers, 36 young people and 16 teachers at both Time 1 and Time 2. Comparison with scores at Time 1 showed that parents reported significantly improved Total Problem scores and Internalizing and Externalizing Problem scores (Table 19). Young people themselves reported significant improvement on The Total Problem scores and on Internalizing Problems, but not on Externalizing Problems. The improved Internalizing scores may be related to the improvements already noted above in the abused children's depressed feelings and their self-esteem. By contrast, teachers did not report significant change, but the numbers of teachers' reports is small and this must affect the reliability of these particular results.

Table 19 **Parents', teachers' and youth's scores on the Child Behavior Checklist: change between the beginning and end of treatment**

	(n)	Z	two-tailed p
Parents' ratings			
Total Problem scores	(55)	4.24	<.001
Internalizing scores	(55)	2.47	<.02
Externalizing scores	(55)	3.17	<.002
Teachers' ratings			
Total Problem scores	(16)	0.44	ns
Internalizing scores	(16)	1.09	ns
Externalizing scores	(16)	1.38	ns
Victims' self-ratings			
Total Problem scores	(36)	2.83	<.005
Internalizing scores	(36)	3.25	<.002
Externalizing scores	(36)	0.71	ns

There were signs that the relationship between the original Children Depression Inventory (CDI) scores and the CBCL scores observed at Time 1, had remained at Time 2. Children reporting high CDI at Time 1 were significantly more likely to report higher Total Problem, Internalizing Problem and Externalizing Problems at Time 2 (t-value=2.73, 2-tail p .01; t-value=2.80, 2-tail p .009; and t-value=2.19, 2-tail p .036, respectively).

Forecasting Longterm Outcome

Those in charge of the victims' therapies were asked to assess, at the end of treatment, the longer-term outcome for each child. This assessment was available for 59 children only. The comments, which were often detailed, were rated by the researchers as 'poor', 'very poor', 'fair', 'good' and 'very good'. Because of the small numbers, the first two and the last two categories were amalgamated, giving three groups: 'good', 'fair' and 'poor'.

There was no relationship between the forecast group a child was put into at the end of treatment and any of the major likely predictors of longer term outcome noted at the start of treatment. Thus there was no relationship with total needs or specific needs (e.g., the absence of effective parenting skills) identified at Time 1, with the child's self-reported depressive mood, self-esteem, age at referral or gender, maternal depressed mood (either GHQ or BDI scores), or measures of severity of abuse. With one exception, there was no relationship either with any of these variables measured at Time 2. The exception was the total score for 'needs' identified at Time 2, where the more needs were identified the worse the centre worker's prediction. However, it is obvious that this is highly tautological: if the centre worker notes a large number of outstanding needs in the child, the family and the parents, it is not surprising that they then take a pessimistic view of long-term outcome. Conversely, where they noted few outstanding needs, they took a positive view of the longer term. It is noteworthy that at Time 2 these 'needs' and the prediction of outcome appear to bear no relationship to any other measures, either standardised or 'soft'. One must again bear in mind, however, the large number of children for whom there were no data at Time 2.

Outcome for the mothers of victims

Only 52 mothers of victims completed self-report questionnaires at Time 2. Overall scores are, however, less important than the extent of change, and only 45 had also completed Time 1 questionnaires. There was no significant change in the mothers' GHQ scores, nor in the subscores: nearly as many women's GHQ scores increased (16) as decreased (18), while the rest were the same as Time 1 (Table 20). Their Beck Depression Inventory scores also did not show significant change: 19 women's scores decreased and 19 increased (with two the same) (Table 20). In contrast, the self-esteem scores of 29 women had improved significantly over the period of their children's treatment, while the scores of 12 women declined. We have noted that maternal scores were not related to the centre workers' predictions of a good, fair or poor long-term outcome for the child.

Table 20 **The extent of change in mothers' self-report scores between the start and end of their children's treatment**

Self-report measure	(n)	Z	2-tailed p
General Health Questionnaire	(45)	1.25	.21 (ns)
Beck Depression Inventory	(40)	1.02	.31 (ns)
Self-esteem Inventory	(41)	2.65	.008

The two groups of 'needs' identified at the start of their child's treatment were rated again for 66 mothers at the end of treatment. Table 21 shows that parents' own needs were judged to have diminished significantly, but their parenting needs did not show such marked changes.

Table 21 **Extent of change in needs identified for parents at the start and end of their children's treatment**

Area of identified needs	(n)	Z	2-tailed p
Parent's own needs	(66)	2.00	.045
parenting skills	(66)	.58	.56 (ns)

Part 2

The Young Perpetrators and their Mothers

We have already reported that only 17 young perpetrators completed treatment within the timescale of the study. In one centre almost all the boys dropped out before the end of the treatment programme, and could not be contacted thereafter; they could not therefore be included in the Time 2 material. In other centres, boys had not completed their treatment, although they were still attending. Information was given by the centres for 19 boys on how many sessions they had completed: the number ranged from 2 to 30.

The numbers with completed treatment are therefore too small to do more than indicate the direction of changes on the standardised questionnaires.

The Effects of Therapeutic Intervention

Children's Depression Inventory (CDI)

At the end of treatment only 17 boys filled in the CDI, but two of these had not completed the questionnaire at Time 1. Comparison of scores at the start and end of treatment (Time 1 and Time 2 respectively) was therefore only possible for 15 boys. The small numbers meant that statistical tests were inappropriate, and proportions only are given in Table 22.

By the end of the year (Time 3), only nine boys filled in the CDI again. A small number of these boys (4/9) improved their scores from Time 1 to Time 3, but for four more there was no change over the year. One boy's score had deteriorated.

The self-esteem inventory

Scores were available after treatment for 14 boys: nine boys indicated higher self-esteem, while four were worse, and one the same.

Blame Attribution Inventory

Like the other self-report scores the Blame Attribution Inventory scores did not show substantial change. Total scores, and the three sub-scores (labelled guilt, external and mental) all remained much as they had been at the start of treatment.

Table 22 **Self-Reported improvement at the end of treatment**

	(n)	better	worse	same
Children's Depression Inventory	(15)	6	7	2
Blame Inventory	(15)	7	4	4
Self-esteem Inventory	(14)	9	4	1

Clinically identified needs

The identified 'needs' were recorded for 17 boys, and none of these showed significant change over the period of treatment. However, this was almost certainly a product of the fact that so many boys were rated as having no 'needs at the point of referral, that the opportunity for registering improvement with this measure was removed.

The Child Behavior Checklist (CBCL)

Child Behavior Checklist scores were available for small numbers, which meant that the results could not be assessed by conventional statistics. Parents' scores were available for 12 boys, and showed reasonably high proportions with improvement on Internalizing, Externalizing and Total Problems scores (Table 23). It should be noted that nine of the 'improved' boys attended one treatment centre in Northern Ireland, showing the effectiveness of that particular programme (at least in the short-term). Fourteen boys reported Time 2 CBCL scores: only about half the boys reported improvement on any of the scales. Teacher scores were available for only eight boys.

Table 23 **Changes observed in the scores obtained from the Child Behavior Checklists (Parent, Teacher and Youth Self-Report) for young perpetrators**

	(n)	better	worse	same
Parents				
Total Problem scores	(12)	9	2	1
Internalizing scores	(12)	9	2	1
Externalizing scores	(12)	10	2	–
Teachers				
Total Problem scores	(8)	7	6	1
Internalizing scores	(8)	7	6	1
Externalizing scores	(8)	7	7	–
Youth				
Total Problem scores	(14)	3	4	1
Internalizing scores	(14)	5	1	2
Externalizing scores	(14)	2	3	3

It is interesting to note that at the second administration of the Youth Self-Report, boys scored significantly higher (i.e., worse) on the Total Problem and Internalizing Problem scores when their original actions had included penetrative rather than non-contact or contact/non-penetrative abuse (t-value=2.70, 2-tail significance=.022; and t-value=3.28, 2-tail significance=.008, respectively).

The Effects of Therapeutic Intervention on Mothers

Changes in mothers' self-report scores over time

The extent of self-reported change for the mothers of young perpetrators could only be tested on 13 cases where there were questionnaires available at Time 1 and Time 2. Table 24 shows that among these 13 mothers, several improved their scores during treatment, but with such small numbers statistical tests are inappropriate. It appears that the sub-scores of anxiety and somatic symptoms showed the greatest improvement. The BDI, also completed by 13 mothers, with its strong focus on depressive symptoms, did not show much evidence of significant change.

Table 24 **Improvement in self-report scores of mothers of young perpetrators**

Self-report measure	(n)	better	worse	same
General Health Questionnaire	(13)	8	1	4
Anxiety sub-score	(13)	11	1	1
Somatic symptoms s/score	(13)	10	1	2
Social dysfunction s/score	(13)	7	1	4
Depression sub-score	(13)	5	2	6
Beck Depression Inventory	(13)	5	4	4
Self-esteem scores	(13)	7	4	1

Clinically identified needs of mothers

Centre workers had provided comments on the needs of very few (16) of the mothers at Time 1 and again at Time 2. For the majority of these mothers there was no entry on their own needs or their parenting skills at either time, so the figures are not reliable enough to report here.

Chapter 7

Talking to Centre Managers

The opportunity was taken, after the research commitment had ended, to talk to some of the centre managers (team leaders) and a very few centre workers about the difficulties and advantages to them of the evaluation project.

Unfortunately, it was not possible to see all centre managers, and the following section covers comments from a selection (but hopefully a fair selection) of the managers. We have also drawn on comments made to us during the study, either when the centres were visited and researchers asked to be told about difficulties, or raised in letters, or raised in the collection of general information about the work of the centres.

Setting up the Centres and their Services

The centres varied in how financially secure the managers felt they were, and in the difficulties they had encountered in setting up the services for sexually abused children, or young perpetrators. Some were well integrated into the local authorities' structures, with which they may have worked for years. Some worked only with one Local Authority, some worked with many, with different expectations and working practices.

Financial uncertainty was sometimes reflected in uncertainty about the aims of the organisation, and therefore about who the service was intended for, or even what service should be provided. Obviously, the larger children's charities tended not to face these difficulties, but even here, managers pointed to major setting-up difficulties, ranging from obtaining planning permission for the treatment centre, building work, and (most importantly) becoming known locally as a service provider for a particular group of children. Uncertainty about the viability of a centre had implications for the recruitment of well-trained and experienced therapeutic staff, who sometimes had only short-term contracts. As one manager said: 'There wasn't much competition for the posts!'

At the start of this Report we pointed out that the numbers of children going into, or not going into specialist treatment after victimisation, or being identified as a young perpetrator, are not known. Even at the local level, centre managers did not have a clear picture of the numbers of children that they might be asked to provide the specialist service for, or for whom their service was appropriate. Their only recourse was to 'put the word about' when they first set up a centre, or started a new service. Networking was an essential part of the centre manager's job, and not always easy. The general impression both they and we had was that there were far more children who could benefit from their services than were being routed through to the Centres, but the figures to support this were not available. The actual numbers that appeared for assessment or treatment were enormously varied, even though the populations might appear very similar. In a not dissimilar period, one centre had over 300 referrals, another had 40. The development of Children's Services Plans (now a mandatory requirement) may make it easier for individual centres to plan ahead.

Some centres were expected to fit their sexual abuse victim work around the generalised support for families in extreme need who were their traditional clients. One FSU had

> 'no child sexual abuse (csa) team as such, but we have always done csa work at the same time as our other work. Part of our group work will be for sexually abused boys and girls, because of the interest among the staff.'

This manager and his workers recognised the lack of good facilities in their building, in which there were very severe constraints on space. They would like more play space, and rooms for individual work.

Changes in local authority responsibilities and the chance for them to 'buy in' specialised services, offered opportunities to these voluntary agency centres, but also left them exposed to market-type forces. They might (and did) lose contracts as well as gain them, but it appeared that the expectations of the contract was usually expressed as 'numbers to be treated' rather than numbers improved, so there was considerable pressure on managers to push cases through. In this centre, the manager felt that only recently had one of the feeder local authorities got on top of proper assessment to see which children would benefit from the specialist work, while another had always specified exactly the number of session: 'three for Jonny and family; twelve for the Bloggs sisters'. This implies good communication, with the centre being explicit about the nature of their therapy and the local authority being clear about the levels of need of individual clients.

An inevitable tension lay in the fact that some therapists were sometimes reluctant to let a child or family go, when they felt that further work could make yet greater improvements. Other therapists were reluctant to say what work they would be doing (and so how long it might take) when they did not know much about the family. Here, there was no treatment 'programme' as such, but rather

> 'sessions flowed out of previous work, and no specific targets were set from the start. As an example, one abused girl clearly had no 'voice' in the family. Early session concentrated wholly on establishing her voice, from which work on her other needs could flow.'

Some managers spoke of the fact that therapists saw their work as being in 'bites' of an established length, perhaps 6 or 12 months; anything less was unthinkable. In other words their work was driven, not so much by the clients' needs, as by some more inflexible vision of a minimum necessary period of treatment. One manager explained that this had rapidly changed, and 3–4 month Review Sessions were held with the clients and the local authorities. In such sessions, therapists described where they had started, the aims and completed work, and the changes to the clients and families. It was surprising that this centre was one which had some of the greatest difficulty in persuading therapists to adhere to the evaluation plan.

In addition, one centre manager said that it was difficult for his centre to be self-financing with therapy only, but his therapists were reluctant to embark on the fee-generating work of court reports, assessments, etc. In fewer than 5% of their cases did the therapists see the child's and family's needs in the same terms as the local authority which was paying for their attendance. This lack of agreement worked both ways: sometimes the therapists wished to stop work, but keep open the option of picking it up later, if necessary, while the local authority wanted work to carry the family through to new heights of competence, which therapists saw as wholly unrealistic. One of the FSU centre managers said that his local authority did not ask the centre to work on sexual abuse issues. They were asked to provide for families with massive problems, among which sexual abuse often figured. He questioned whether dealing only with sexual abuse was a 'healthy' workload. He also considered that it increased professional skills to be able to work with perpetrators as well as victims.

As one manager put it: 'Initially the work was driven by the needs of the children, later by their needs *and* by finance'. He also stated: 'The therapists, who were very good at their job, were not good at managing their time in a financial sense. It grated on those not used to making financial judgments.'

Selection of Cases

When it came to the selection of cases, some centres reported that they would not take on very disturbed or violent children whether they were abused or abusing. There was also an understandable reluctance to accept suicidal cases, although this sat awkwardly with the fact that many workers said they were uncomfortable with including a question on suicidal ideation in the children's questionnaires. Most centres did not work with young people over the age of 18, although one centre accepted a 20-year old young woman with some learning difficulties.

Early in the study the centre managers were asked to provide information on the numbers of cases they had seen in 1991 and projections for 1992 (when the current study began). Figures were made available from only six centres. In view of the cases subsequently fed through to the research project the figures reported by these managers were optimistic. For example, one centre reported an expectation of 'treating' 63 cases, but only fed 8 into the current project; figures for a second centre were 12 expected young perpetrators, but only one was fed into the project; a third centre expected 124 sexually abused children in treatment, but eventually only 14 were included in the current study. Set against these apparent reductions in numbers, one centre reported that they might 'treat' 12 cases in 1992, but in the end saw over 20.

Staffing

Most of the centre staff were social workers, but some centres had the benefit of multi-disciplinary teams, which might include part-time clinical psychologists, art therapists, play therapists and child psychiatrists. One centre employed psychotherapists. One FSU manager said that no-one on the staff had specific training; 'we have trained ourselves in sexual abuse work'. But with two leading paediatric specialists in child abuse working locally, one of whom was on the management team of the centre, this FSU had been 'educated' in the field. And he pointed out that sexual abuse was only one experience in the generally chaotic families about which the unit was very experienced.

In one centre the manager emphasised that the work done with "chaotic" families without boundaries had become more focused in the last ten years [one third of the caseload in 1982 had been 'on the books' for 10 years or more]. Information on sexual abuse which is now more frequently available than it had been ten years ago, had improved the quality of this centre's work with such families.

Understanding the Purposes of Evaluation

There was no lack of understanding about what evaluation was. One manager expressed this well:

> 'Evaluation is about assessing the value of work that been done—
> both critical and positive—to better serve the needs of families
> and children in the future.'

However, another manager stressed that, while evaluation would show whether a positive outcome followed particular programmes of help, this meant that therapists had to be clear about the contents of the programme. He expressed a number of doubts about whether the therapists would be able to describe with complete clarity what their aims were, and how they carried out their work.

Carrying out the Evaluation Project

The commitment, both of centre managers and of their staff, varied considerably across the 18 Centres. While many staff appeared to be pleased with the notion of evaluation, their commitment to carrying out the *tasks* of evaluation was not always present: as one manager said, 'Basically, people did not do what they were asked'. A number of explanations for the variations were put forward, which are detailed in the Discussion below.

In part explanation it is worth emphasising that, when the researchers embarked on the work, they assumed that each Centre had self-selected into the project, and that all workers would be equally committed. Head offices had been guided in their choice of centres by a number of considerations, but commitment of all the centre staff was clearly not one of them. There is nothing inherently wrong with this situation, but the preparation for the evaluation project should have taken this into account. Unfortunately, the researchers had only allowed for minimum preparation and introduction time, when in fact each centre really needed a lot more help initially and throughout in order to keep staff committed and comfortable with the ideas behind evaluation and the tasks it demanded. The geographical spread (see Appendix A) did not help.

This was well expressed by one manager:

> 'It's very difficult to incorporate something which is dictated into something which has evolved. It was not just getting the therapists to fill things in, but getting them to hold onto the notion. It quickly slipped away. I tried everything, including big reminder notices around the building, with Department of Health on them!'

or another:

> 'It (the evaluation) felt like an option or add-on, but should have been integral.'

In contrast to this perspective, one manager, asked if the centre would have adopted some sort of evaluation of children's progress without the current project, replied that they would not, and that they needed to be *told* to do it to see any advantages.

Managers were very realistic in their criticisms: one manager wrote:

> 'As you know, we are doing our best to cooperate with the research but are experiencing some difficulties; not the least that it is very time consuming *and* it is not always easy from a therapeutic angle to intorduce the questionnaire when the family is not very well or engaged with us'

Set against these difficulties, some managers reported advantages. For example one said:

> 'I think it was useful to have the discipline of therapists filling in the data sheets, though it took some doing. The process of referring back to filled-in questionnaires was very beneficial. One of our foster parents said: 'Hasn't my view of them (the children) changed!'
>
> 'It would be nice to know if the management of the sexual abuse problems had produced changes in the child's behaviour, which was the only thing the local authority were interested in.'

One manager reported gaining new insights into family functioning when he visited the children's own homes to get the data sheets filled in and administered the questionnaires. He also felt that using one person to supervise the filling in of questionnaires probably improved the consistency of approach to helping and explaining. He also pointed to the potential for better management accountability.

The Method of Evaluation

Both method and measures used in the evaluation came in for criticism. Against the background that few workers had experience of systematic data collection, or of using questionnaires, their comments are nevertheless to be respected.

The measures were criticised for format and language. In particular the double negatives of several self-esteem questions were felt to make things very difficult for some children and mothers. Some managers also criticised the administration of so many questionnaires, and their re-administration often only a few weeks later.

Setting up their own Evaluation Systems

Since managers mentioned finding it difficult to organise (and sometimes to support) external evaluation, they were asked whether they would have run their own, if their head offices had not agreed to the external research. Few would have done, but those that considered that they might, emphasised that the advantage would have been that they would have 'owned' the results. One manager said they would have been able to phrase the questions more suited to their own needs, but agreed after discussion that these would have included many of the issues covered either by the Child Behavior Checklists or the Identification of Needs.

> 'Put like that, I can see we missed an opportunity to use these parts of the evaluation to help ourselves.'

However, he did add that:

> 'Being pragmatic, the therapists wouldn't have done it even if we'd started it. It was difficult enough for them to separate the Reviews (held at 3 month intervals) from therapy, they were reluctant about them. Largely because they felt that by committing a view to paper, it would become the truth about that child, but another felt that since reality changed so frequently, there was no point in committing to paper anyway.'

Another manager pointed out the dangers of writing down clinical judgments, in the present climate of uncertainty, and 'harassment' of social workers in sexual abuse cases.

The issues identified as important by this manager were: monitoring behaviour, recording further victimisation, possibly self-esteem issues.

Asking about evaluation systems at the start of the current project, it was clear that, by-and-large, this loosely meant finding out how the young people were getting on: phrases such as 'Feedback from participants and families. One Centre held three or four meetings with the whole group of young perpetrators at six monthly meetings to review 'progress and welfare'; although there was no mention of systematic recording of progress, there is no doubt that this length of follow-up must be an effective way of monitoring the cases.

For some teams evaluation meant monitoring the on-going therapeutic work, and longer-term evaluation of the effects of treatment on the clients was not seen as a necessary part of the therapy. This, of course, raises the question of which bodies, if any, should carry this responsibility. Several managers reported that there were simply no arrangements for post-treatment follow-up; and, specifically, their centre was not funded to do this work.

Some centre managers saw the place of evaluating the children's progress as contributing to designing improved services.

One manager, whose centre had reached a stage of reviewing the work with sexually abused children and their families, saw the need for more flexibility in order to meet the demands of local authorities, including short, intensive residential work with some abused children and their families.

Chapter 8

Discussion and Recommendations

This study was set up to monitor the progress made by sexually abused children and young perpetrators of sexual abuse through community-based voluntary agency special programmes. Many of the original aims were only partially achieved, sometimes for reasons well outside the control of either researchers or centre workers. However, the need to provide better information on the effectiveness of treatment available to the two groups of children and adolescents we studied remains as important as ever. It is our firm belief that our results provide clear pointers to ways in which the practice of assessing the progress of these two groups may be improved. Below we discuss some of the difficulties that were encountered, their possible causes, and outline how systems might be changed to give clearer answers in future.

Before discussing the difficulties, however, we would draw attention to the fact that the aims of the current study were similar to those outlined as appropriate to the current (poor) level of knowledge about young perpetrators by the NCH Committee of Enquiry (1992). The research recommendations of this Committee covered many of the points we highlight below as persistent barriers to good evaluation both for abused children and young perpetrators, indicating that there is still a long way to go before we have the answers we need to how well abused and abusive children and adolescents do in the current child-care climate.

It is important also to draw attention again to the apparently very low take-up of the services provided by the Centres included in the current study. Will (1995), reporting on the first five years of a specialist service in Edinburgh for adolescent sex offenders, expressed dismay that the average of 10.5 referrals each year was 'surprisingly low'.

Difficulties Encountered in the Research

In discussing some of the difficulties we encountered in the research project we need to emphasise the enthusiasm of the majority of centre workers about the idea of evaluating the progress of the children. Doubts were expressed by some individuals, but overall the research project was greeted warmly in the initial stages. For some centre workers enthusiasm only waned when they realised the extent of what they were being asked to do. Later, when they were being "chased" by their own team leaders, administrators and the research team to complete schedules, many centre workers appeared to find it difficult to put a high priority on this work. It is therefore worth considering the reasons why some centre workers found that they could not sustain their earlier commitment. In doing so, it is important to state that the following discussion is not intended to be critical of individuals, but to simply highlight the difficulties which we have observed, and to enable teams to approach evaluation in more positive ways.

We have identified four main reasons why many centre workers appeared to have difficulty either in sustaining their commitment to evaluation, or setting a high enough value on it to ensure completion of the work. In reviewing these reasons, we would emphasise that we are not alone in meeting various forms of (perhaps unconscious) resistance to evaluating intervention. Wiffen (1994), among others, is quoted as saying that social workers tend to be 'defensive and uncertain about what evaluation is for', and Huxley (1994) has pointed to a general reluctance on the part of UK social workers to accept the need for evaluation, compared with their colleagues in the US. The full range of objections which are frequently cited by social workers are summarised by Huxley (1994) in his paper comparing attitudes to outcome research in Colorado, USA and the UK.[9] Parker et al (1992) also noted that there was widespread resistance by child care practitioners (particularly social workers) to introducing more systematic measurement of children's progress through the intervention procedures. The list of difficulties cited by Parker and colleagues were reproduced in more than one centre with which we worked. For example, systematically measuring children's psychological and social adjustment, whether by using standardised instruments or semi-structured interviews and checklists, was seen as *always* providing less useful information than a 'case' profile. This may be so for an individual child, but the use of questionnaires can usefully augment what can be got from an interview, and provides both a systematic picture of the groups in treatment, and (if selected with this in mind) can provide substantial evidence of a client's progress. One or two workers recognised this, and said they would probably continue to use the Children's Depression Inventory.

Doubts about and opposition to evaluation included the following:

> i) '**It is really about staff evaluation, and could lead to staff redundancies**': Introducing the evaluation we emphasised that we were not commissioned to comment on the quality of work which was done in the therapeutic centres. Nevertheless, this clearly remained an anxiety, noted also by Wiffen (1994), and this point is important in view of the reportedly low morale among social workers (who formed the largest group of therapists in the centres).

> ii) '**The process of evaluation 'abuses' clients**': Systematic evaluation of clients' progress will probably include administering some

9 This difference between social workers in the USA & Britain should not be exaggerated. Huxley was working in a highly specialised treatment setting. Informal information from US researchers in the field of child abuse & neglect suggests that many US practitioners responsible for service delivery have very similar difficulties to those expressed by child protection workers in the UK.

questionnaires, or using standardized information-getting interviews. Several workers expressed the view that administering questionnaires was 'abusive' to clients. Huxley (1994) has noted that there are deep-seated cultural differences in the attitudes of US and UK professionals to contributing to systematic record-keeping and administering questionnaires. To set against this, a few workers already used self-report from children, and others found that there were clinical advantages from using them. Centre workers also found that some children and adolescents prefer and enjoy paper-and-pencil questionnaires to being asked questions face-to-face, others do not. Multi-disciplinary teams were more likely to use, or to see advantages in using, such variety of approaches.

The letter quoted on page 73 neatly illustrates the dilemma for clinical staff, and the different perspectives they brought to the study compared with researchers. It was widely reported that it was nigh impossible to get questionnaires filled in when the staff did not know the family and/or child very well. In fact the centre workers were remarkably successful in getting the children and adolescents to fill in the self-report questionnaires. They appeared less successful with the mothers.

iii) **'Therapists should not do non-therapeutic tasks, and filling in data-gathering forms is non-therapeutic'**: Centre workers frequently expressed doubts about whether they should spend time on tasks (such as filling in the research data sheets) that did not have immediate therapeutic value for the client. Some centre workers clearly had difficulty foreseeing the advantages of building up large bodies of systematically acquired information in order to gain more understanding about the efficacy of treatments, and in particular the treatments their Centre was offering. Again, Huxley's (1994) point about cultural perspectives is pertinent, but it is also important to acknowledge that such tasks are time-consuming and managers need to make allowance for this.

iv) **'It would have been alright if it had not been imposed from outside'**: This is an important point, which has already been raised in Chapter 7 reporting our conversations with Centre managers. It is one to which we return in our recommendations. Nevertheless, it is also true that many of the projects in the current study, and others like them, have been providing therapeutic intervention for many years, without workers demanding or initiating proper evaluation of their clients' progress be set up. So clearly this problem does not have a straightforward solution. On the face of it, it would appear that such centres do not evaluate their own work, until required to do so from 'outside'.

The Purposes of Evaluation

In view of the concerns, anxieties and problems felt by so many centre workers we consider it important to describe what is meant by evaluation and to review the advantages and disadvantages of evaluation.

Evaluation in the context of the current study means prospectively tracking the progress (or lack of progress) of each centre's clients over a wide range of measures, chosen at least partly to reflect the reasons for the client's referral. When centre workers had difficulties with the current project, it was seldom with the principle of evaluation, but with the means for achieving it.

The main purpose of evaluation must be to improve, where it is necessary, the services which are being provided. The point has been well made that evaluation is a client's right: confirmation that the service is always aiming to improve in ways which affect what is available to him or her (Wiffen, 1994; Newman, 1994). We have seen that this point was made by at least one Project Manager in the final interview with the researchers. This must be particularly important in fields like sexual abuse, where much of the practice is relatively new. To achieve this, information must be available to practitioners which enable them to assess whether their service achieves the therapeutic targets they have themselves set, as well as those set by others. Evaluation also enables professionals to get a clearer idea of what happens to clients as they progress through treatment and in the following months and years.

The NCH Committee of Enquiry (1992) also pointed to other advantages arising from improved information about sexual abuse cases:

- How many children and young people need help?
- What is the significance of background variables?
- What sexual behaviour could be regarded as 'harmless', or within the 'normal' range for any given age-group?
- What treatment methods and approaches are most effective?

The current study was not set up to answer these questions, not least because it had access to a highly selected group, namely those whose sexual abuse or sexually abusive behaviour had already been discovered, and whose cases had been processed through to therapeutic intervention. As we noted in our introduction, only a proportion of cases reach this stage, and at present it is not known how many. Some of the points we raise below about evaluating outcome of cases which enter therapeutic programmes, could as well be applied to other organisations responsible for earlier stages in the careers of sexual abuse cases. All the questions raised in the NCH report share a requirement that specific information is collected systematically. If cases drop out of the 'system' of discovery, enquiry, assessment, treatment and outcome re-assessment it is increasingly urgent that they be formally identified as having dropped out.

Thorpe (1994) states that 'In child protection, . . . patterns are not self-evident' and therefore need systematic analysis to be discovered. If we accept the evidence of this study and the points made by Huxley (1994), then it appears there are many practitioners treating abused children and young perpetrators of sexual abuse who are not able to draw on systematic evidence when they wish to review the overall effectiveness of their own work. It is likely, therefore, that practitioners are vulnerable to fashions in treatment, rather than empirically tested models.

It has been said that 'Outcomes in child protection are indeterminate' (Noyes, 1993), but they will remain so unless the problems around measuring outcomes are tackled. We would suggest that there are ways in which that 'indeterminate' outcome can be clarified: some of these are addressed by Gibbons et al (1995b).

Huxley (1994) has suggested that one possible reason why evaluation was more readily accepted in the US than in the UK was that funding was frequently dependent on evaluation having already taken place. The monies appeared to come as a reward, rather than an inducement. In the present financial climate of community-based family intervention work in the UK, such an arrangement is hard to conceive unless that systematic collection of data is understood to be an integral part of the service. More typically, in the current study some, but not all, centres received some extra funding specifically to collaborate in the monitoring programme. Many centres felt that they did not receive any reward in return for the extra administrative burden of processing the children and families into the present study. In all cases where there was some extra funding, it appeared before rather than after the research study, but was not tied to how the evaluation would be achieved. Thus, it went into expanding the teams working with sexually abused children or young perpetrators, rather than into addressing the issues within the centres of how the evaluation could be achieved. [An exception to this was the work of NCH on developing a new data base for these clients.] There was a danger, therefore, that evaluation was seen as the responsibility of the external researchers alone.

Huxley (1994) also noted that, in the US programme, feedback from evaluation provided rewards for project workers. Unfortunately, this was not possible in the current study, partly because of the small numbers recorded by individual centres (which could not provide reliable information for programme evaluation), and partly because the large amount of missing data invalidated much of the analysis. Although it is an obvious point, it is important to emphasise that the reward can only come *after* the monitoring work, and the form the reward takes (that the children get 'better' or, if they do not, that programmes can be revised) cannot be predicted. There is, therefore an element of investment and risk in undertaking evaluation of clients' progress.

Evaluation can also provide a better picture of the referred groups, as well as their responses to intervention. In turn, this increases the knowledge of the extent and persistence of symptoms, behaviour difficulties and outstanding personal needs. In certain circumstances, evaluation can feed into staff development and service delivery. It is worth emphasising that to put effective evaluation systems in place will ensure that more attention is given to what is a desirable outcome—a relatively neglected issue in child protection at present (Browne, 1993). For example, while it is a desirable outcome to provide a child with an environment in which she does not encounter abuse, it may (in the long-run) be more desirable to give that child the skills and attitudes which will enable her to deal with abusive situations as they arise. To return to the issue of 'grooming', if the abused child is not helped to overcome the effects of grooming she will remain vulnerable to new sex offenders, even if meanwhile she has been 'rescued' from the original abuser.

Setting Evaluation Systems in Place

For evaluation to be useful to centres and organisations various issues clearly need to be addressed at the time the systems are put in place. We would emphasise that good clinical practice and good research share aims and techniques; for example, in both cases there is a concern with constantly improving the knowledge base, and drawing conclusions from new information. Even so Parker et al (1992) found that systematic measuring of children's (psychological) progress was not seen as an integral part of good clinical practice (p 42). Waterman & Lusk (1993) have argued that, while psychological testing of children may have limited value in establishing that sexual abuse has taken place, such tests are useful in clinical work, a point which was also made to the researchers by several centre workers. In addition, Waterman & Lusk noted that while differences between sexually abused children and others are often not significant on tests administered to children, parents' reports show marked differences.

Lonnqvist (1984) has given a diagrammatic representation of the organisation of systematic evaluation, reproduced below (Figure 12). In this schema it can be seen that the treatment process, the information systems and the evaluation are inextricably linked.

Figure 12
Achieving systematic evaluation of treatment

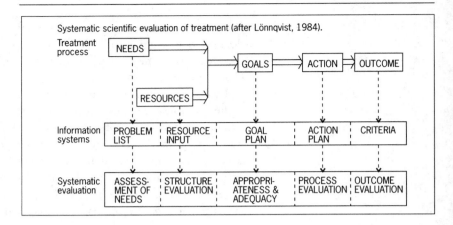

Systematic scientific evaluation of treatment (after Lönnqvist, 1984).

Taken from F. Almqvist, The Challenge of Evaluation of Intervention. In M. H. Schmidt & H. Remschmidt, (Eds), Needs and Prospects of Child and Adolescent Psychiatry. (pp 179–183). With permission: Hogrefe & Huber, Publishers, Stuttgart.

The Implications of Evaluation for the Child Protection Professionals

Arising from the present study, it appeared to us that it is essential to ensure more *systematic ways of recording* the basic information about the family demography, the abuse experiences and/or the abusive actions of the referred children and young people. Only when this has been done for several years over a large number of therapeutic programmes will a more accurate picture of the young abused populations be established, and vital questions on outcome of treatment be answered. The same point is, of course, true for young perpetrator populations.

We acknowledge that, as Huxley (1994) has pointed out, there will need to be a change of professional attitudes to evaluation and the tasks which go with it. Describing the acceptance of standardised outcome measures by the teams responsible for young children's welfare in Colorado, Huxley points out that 'careful selection and use of standardized measures for outcome purposes can be done by professionals working with children and families, as part of on-going practice and service evaluation'. We need therefore to be clear about what such evaluation will entail. Below we make some suggestions, but would direct those embarking on evaluation to the work of Pietrzak, Ramler, Renner, et al (1990). For more advanced analysis of data on young sex offenders, the review by Furby, Weinrott & Blackshaw (1989) provides useful advice.

i What questions need answers?

The first stage in the organisation is to set down the questions to which answers are needed. From this will emerge the type and sources of information which are needed to provide the answers, and the timescale for obtaining the data. There are no short-cuts to getting the answers, but this groundwork makes the strategies clear. These issues are exceptionally well laid out in Pietrzak et al (1990). To give one obvious example, evaluating interventions with depressed and suicidal teenagers would require some measurement of those particular symptoms, although information on self-esteem or family relationships would also be of interest. This may appear as obvious to some readers, but it will be recalled that several workers expressed grave doubts about even asking the children about suicidal thoughts.

ii Choosing measures to answer questions

The literature on sexual abuse provides some guidance to the measures which might be appropriate for evaluating the progress of abused children, or of young perpetrators. Some assessments may be appropriate to both groups (e.g., behaviour or conduct disorders, or Attention Deficit Hyperactivity Disorders—ADHD), while others are likely to apply to the first rather than the second group (e.g., Post Traumatic Stress Disorder—PTSD).

To some extent, the choice of measures to assess sexually abused children has to be dependent on the make-up of the clinical team. For example, diagnosis of child and adolescent psychiatric disorders (e.g., PTSD) cannot be established without trained psychiatrists or clinical psychologists. But while it may not be possible to give a diagnosis of PTSD, it will be possible to establish the extent of PTSD symptoms with the use of checklists, such as 38-item Symptom Checklist (Conte, Berliner & Schuerman, 1986). A wide range of symptoms and behaviour disturbance can be assessed by such self- and other-report questionnaires as the Child Behavior Checklist (Achenbach & Edlebrock, 1983; Achenbach, 1991).

However, it has to be admitted that many of the key issues in sexual perpetration (e.g., accepting responsibility for the abusive acts, reducing distorted cognitions around sexual matters) are hard to measure reliably, and more work is needed in these areas.

Parker and his colleagues (1992) have reviewed the ways in which child care practitioners should monitor the psychosocial development of children in the UK childcare system, and have suggested that current practice does not serve the best interests of children and their families. The importance of a developmental perspective has also been emphasised by Berliner (1991). Any systematic evaluation of children and adolescents and subsequent tracking of their progress must be set against expectations appropriate for their age, gender and development.

iii Letting other agencies know any new requirements

Some parts of the data-gathering may have an impact on other agencies, for example, in the type of information they need to supply.

We would also suggest that therapeutic agencies, like the ones with which we worked, should be able to insist that the referrer pass on all relevant information. In the cases involving children, particularly sexual abuse cases, there is an obvious advantage—not to mention an ethnical responsibility—in not subjecting the child or other traumatised members of the family to yet another interview to collect 'the facts' of the case (Dobson, 1994). Even with this very reasonable expectations, many centres were working with very limited information about the background to the abuse.

iv Record-keeping

Any organisation intending to evaluate their intervention work will have to adopt some measure of standardised record-keeping. We have already noted that some reluctance was expressed in the current study about the need for standardised record-keeping. But it is increasingly accepted that some standardisation of records is a necessary part of good practice when working with abused or at risk children (e.g., Social Services Inspectorate report on Islington Social Services Dept. July 1994). In a recent inspection of local authorities' child protection services, SSI commented that none of the authorities had guidelines on record keeping, and the quality of records was 'generally poor'. SSI stated that this issue needs 'urgent attention' (SSI, 1994). We would echo this sentiment and suggest that the issue needs to be incorporated into professional in-service training, and initial training.

In relation to therapeutic programmes for young perpetrators, Ross & Loss (1991) have emphasised that the assessment of the young sex offender serves (among other purposes) to define the treatment goals. The assessment should therefore incoporate measures which will provide clear information on the successful achievement of those goals.

Thorpe (1994) has also pointed out that there must be a 'longitudinal dimension' in any record-keeping system, which in turn produces important measures of outcome. The question of what to standardise (which means insisting both that it is recorded for all clients, and that it is recorded in the same way) emerges naturally from addressing our first point: what information is needed to answer what questions?

v Building in the time for data-gathering

In the present study, the centre workers frequently pointed out that they did not have the time to fill in more forms or help clients to complete questionnaires. Some of the issues around time reflected unfamiliarity with collecting relevant data. For example, despite the Training and Information days in which researchers introduced the research project, many centre workers continued to believe that they must take children and parents through the self-report questionnaires line by line, even when they were competent readers. One centre worker described the time taken to "interview" a child, and this turned out to mean that he had spent one and a half hours discussing the child's responses to each item of the Children's Depression Inventory: a child who can read should normally be able to complete this 27-item leaflet in about 10–15 minutes. Not surprisingly, this child refused to complete the other questionnaires in the booklet.

This was a well-meant attempt by the centre worker to provide 'help' to a troubled client. But the experience of clinicians and researchers alike has shown that paper-and-pencil tests are often completed quite comfortably by troubled children, provided the atmosphere is supportive and they know they can ask for help *if they need it*.

In addition to some reluctance to ensure effective data-gathering, some practitioners may not fully realise that they already have much of the information that is needed in the 'new' system. The difference between an 'old' and a 'new' system may thus simply lie in re-organising how and when the data are recorded. If this is done sensibly, time may in fact be saved. Clasping an enormous file, one worker said he hadn't got time to complete the data booklet, but 10 minutes conversation with the researcher proved that he held much of the information (about family size, ethnicity, etc) in his head, because he knew the child and her family so well.

Alongside the need to give centre workers time and support to collect the data systematically on current cases, there are questions to be asked about who should be responsible for the longer-term follow-up of cases. To be most useful to centre workers, data are needed about the long-term outcome of their cases, but it is not possible to conduct long-term follow-up studies in the present climate of financial constraints. Inevitably, professionals in this field must concentrate limited resources on intervention and treatment. So whose responsibility is it to find out how the clients do in the long-term?

vi *The implications of evaluation for clients*

Undertaking evaluation may have some impact on clients. Most importantly, it suggests the expectation of longer term contact, well after the therapeutic team has 'finished' their work. Clients need to be reassured about confidentiality perhaps to an even greater extent than they might demand about their therapists' records. Evaluation over time may mean asking to visit the family or individual some months or years ahead.

Inevitably, there may be some occasions on which a client (whether individual or family) will be asked for information which is not immediately relevant to their problem: a question to which the answer is 'no' , or 'not applicable'. If the information-gathering interview is described as such, is kept as focused and brief as possible, and the purpose is clearly explained to the clients the large majority will not refuse this 'extra' time. People are used to providing a range of information to doctors, nurses and others in helping or therapeutic 'roles'. The attitude of the person acquiring the routine information is crucial in obtaining consent and cooperation: respect and sensitivity are important, but had, in the present study, also been used to *avoid* asking the clients for any information. One can make no assumptions about what questions individuals find difficult or embarrassing.

Reviewing the Measures used in the Current Study

In the current study the choice of measures and of the information necessary to help establish what progress the children had made was based on literature searches and clinical experience. In some cases it appeared that a questionnaire contributed no new dimension to the overall picture of the sexually abused child: we would not, for example, recommend that the Fears Schedule is useful in this field. Nevertheless, fearfulness is still an important symptom among abused children (Berliner, 1991), but may be better measured as part of the full range of PTSD symptoms.

New measures may also be needed. For example, while it is important to collect information on the type, severity and duration of abuse, and on the relationship between abuser and abused, it is becoming clear that not enough attention has been given to the preliminary grooming experience. Bannister (1994) draws attention to the 'distortions of thought and perception which will have been imposed by the abuser'. These may be better predictors of the long-term deleterious effects than the other abuse variables (such as severity or duration) traditionally reported in research papers, and clearly require further investigation, although measurement of such distortions may be extremely difficult.

It is also clear that much sexual abuse of children takes place against a background of serious family dysfunction, which in turn increases the vulnerability of the child (Mullen et al, 1993). Again, there are arguments for requiring from those involved in therapeutic intervention that they undertake a systematic assessment of family functioning. Berliner (1991) has pointed out that characteristics of the abusive experience explain relatively small mount of the difference in functioning of the abused and non-abused child. Other factors, such as intelligence or parenting skills, and recognition of the full range of a child's functioning (see Parker et al, 1992), may distinguish the survivors from those who are most damaged by the abuse. Evidence is also emerging about the importance of family violence in the backgrounds of young perpetrators.

It was disappointing that centre workers appeared to take little advantage of the section on 'Identified Needs' of the children and their families. An impression was gained from the low response rate that centre workers were inclined to categorise a child as needy by virtue of being sexually abused, rather than investigating the full range of needs which might have preceded the abuse or emerged after disclosure. Sometimes this was the consequence of decisions taken by the referring agency. For example, one eight year-old girl was molested by a local teenager on her way home from school; she struggled free and ran home to her mother, immediately reporting what had happened. Her mother praised her actions and her disclosure and "dealt with" the teenager herself. The line centre worker's description of the girl implied that there were no subsequent symptoms or difficulties. But the mother mentioned this single event to the family social worker, the girl landed up in a group with some very traumatised and symptomatic children, while no further action was taken with the teenager abuser.

Some centre staff told us that they did not realise the weight that was to be attached to the evidence on the children's and young people's psycho-social adjustment recorded in this section. Nevertheless, the thin response was surprising when measured against the content of most treatment programmes. For example, O'Callaghan & Print (1994) identified the following as essential components of their treatment programme for young sex abusers: denial, cognitive distortions, victim awareness, the cycle of abuse, social skills, sex and sexuality and coping strategies. As we have seen, the Needs profiles in the current study suggested that centre workers were unlikely to record such needs for more than a few of the young perpetrators.

Conclusion: Recognising the Need for Increased Accountability

Accountability is one of those buzz-words with as many meanings as the organisations to which it is attached. Undoubtedly, however, the services provided to sexually abused children or to young perpetrators and their families do need to be accountable at several levels. We suggest three considerations below.

- First, the services need to be able to assure the clients (children and their parents and guardians) about quality. To do so, workers need to be constantly re-assessing their own professional skills and given support to improve them. But, in addition, the professionals need to be given the opportunity to find out whether what they offer is effective. In this they need support in collecting and collating the appropriate information.

- Second, the funding organisations need to be confident that their money has been well-spent. For this, it is essential to be able to show the improvement of (at least some of) the abused children, not just count bodies through doors.

- Third, the organisation need to show that the children attending the specialist facilities are in need of help, and are the most in need of help (two different points), which can only be done if systematic assessment of the children is undertaken. This will ensure that children are not referred to expensive and scarce programmes simply because they have *experienced* abuse, but because they can be seen to need the help provided.

Recommendations

Arising from the experience of this outcome study of sexually abused children and young perpetrators we make some recommendations about the direction in which this type of work should develop. The recommendations are intended to help those working therapeutically in a wide range of settings. Some recommendations refer specifically to training issues (both in-service and vocational). In making these recommendations we are referring to all those who are engaged in delivering intervention services in child abuse cases, rather than to any particular profession. In the recommendations about record-keeping in therapeutic teams we retain the principle that first consideration should always be given to the welfare of the child.

We start from the background of Research Priority 9, in the National Research Council (1993) report on child abuse and neglect in the United States: 'High-quality evaluation studies of existing program and service interventions are needed to develop criteria and instrumentation that can help to identify promising developments in the delivery of treatment and prevention services'.

Recommendation 1

Integrating data collection and clinical practice   Time-limited research programmes assessing outcome for these two client groups should be replaced by monitoring systems which are integral to on-going practice. The collection of data suited to monitoring the progress of individuals or families should be the responsibility of practitioners. Exceptions to this general rule would concern research designed to answer very specific questions, such as whether a certain type of intervention is 'better' than another. Researchers might also be employed in the short-term to use an existing data-base for specific studies.

In integrated monitoring, managers and their teams will be able to develop ways of keeping the information systems closely based on the operational work and still fulfil the need for good performance measures (Kearney & Milner, 1994). There is evidence of such systems being implemented, but the pace is, in our view, too slow to meet the needs of clients, professionals and managers, much less answer the questions put by clients.

Recommendation 2

Developing shared record-keeping systems for a common core of information   Organisations involved in child protection work urgently need to develop systems of record-keeping which are shared, not only within the organisation, but also with others.[10] Once it is established, all workers involved with such organisations should be encouraged and/or required to adopt the system.

Consideration should be given by Government to supporting the development of large data-bases on young perpetrators. NOTA[11] have drawn up a data schedule, and associated soft-ware which can be used with sex offenders. With small amendments this could be used with young perpetrators.

Recommendation 3

Further development and integration of measures appropriate to monitoring the progress of abused children, and of young perpetrators   Further work is needed to improve measurement of the preceding factors and outcomes of sexual abuse, for victims, but more especially for young perpetrators. The CBCL, for example, might be more widely used. More attention needs also to be given to issues outside the traditional clinical range: for example, peer relationships and school performance. More attention should be given to ways of recording systematically the 'grooming' experience preceding the experience of being sexually abused, or the development of 'grooming' habits by young perpetrators both of which may be predictive of future experiences and activities.

Recommendation 4

Incorporating in vocational and in-service training an understanding of the need for and purposes of evaluation   In many child care professions evaluation apparently still has overtones of appraisal of the worker. Training child care workers in the purposes of effective evaluation of the service they provide is urgently needed.

---

[10] We emphasise it is the systems, not the records, which we believe should be shared.
[11] NOTA: National Association for the Development of Work with Sex Offenders.

Chapter 9

Conclusions

The first part of this study reported the progress of sexually abused children who attend voluntary agency therapeutic units. They were not selected in any formal sense, and it is not clear how representative the cases might be of all sexually abused children. However, the internal evidence of the study is that referral processes appear to follow very similar lines in different parts of the country, and the results of the study may thus be taken to be typical of children attending such specialist centres. It needs to be remembered that the group was not homogenous in any way, and the numbers were too small to allow in-depth analysis of the outcome of different sub-groups. The second part of the study concerned a much smaller group of young perpetrators of sexual abuse also attending voluntary agency units. The same points about representativeness of the sample apply to this group.

The need to track the progress of children and their non-abusing parents through therapeutic intervention programmes is necessary for several reasons. First, it is not ethically responsible to continue to deliver a programme to children and families unless one can be sure that at least no harm is being done, and preferably that one can demonstrate the opportunity for improvement by substantial numbers of the treated population. Second, it may be that programmes have different efficacy for different clients, and where it is not so effective some changes are needed. Third, professional integrity and development is better supported by accurate information about clients' progress, than by anecdote and 'hunch'. Fourth, in a climate of reduced resources, it is important to be able to demonstrate efficacy, not least for those who do *not* get onto the programme, who have some reassurance that money is not being wasted. Finally, evaluation of progress through therapeutic programmes has implications for further development of theory in the field of child sexual abuse.

In fact, of course, the evaluation of clients' progress is an integral part of good 'clinical' practice. Practitioners often have a good idea about how successful they have been. What is frequently missing is that evaluation is systematic, rather than idiosyncratic, that the information is recorded in a format accessible to the evaluator or researcher and the measures of 'change' or 'success' can reliably be used by other practitioners.

On one specific issue we must record our concern about the fact that many of the children appear to be allocated to therapeutic services without any systematic formulation of their difficulties or what led up to them. It appeared to us that referral agencies were frequently making a 'diagnosis' of sexual abuse, rather than assessing the symptoms and complex family problems which may surround a particular case. Our findings suggest that some children are being fed into the therapeutic programmes without due attention to their need for such specific help. Any mismatch between the children's symptoms and needs is further compounded in some centres by the absence of systematic assessment before treatment. By not recording what characteristics the child shows on entering a programme it is impossible to assess what progress, if any, has been made.

One important lesson emerges from this work. It is less than satisfactory to 'bolt on' the monitoring of the progress of victims or perpetrators and their families through therapeutic interventions than to build in monitoring procedures which can be seen as integral to the clinical work. Time-limited research projects are subject to many difficulties: for example, if the development of a therapeutic service suffers any slippage it may not be possible to follow all the recipients of that service through to the end of their treatment (this was true for most children in the present study).

We would strongly suggest that there should be a move away from relying on time-limited 'external' research projects to provide answers on progress in treatment and towards an understanding that monitoring the progress of clients is not only integral to service delivery, but also fully the responsibility of the providers of the service. After each treatment group has undertaken to build their own data base of cases assessed, treated and followed up, external or internal researchers can be given access in order to answer specific questions.

We recognise that in the field of child sexual abuse, any one community-based centre is unlikely to see a large number of cases each year, and the feedback from monitoring may appear to diminish. It is at this point that multi-centre co-ordination can be undertaken. Within the large voluntary agencies, such as NSPCC or Action for Children (NCH), centres can be asked to contribute a common database. The NSPCC, for example, has a history of maintaining records from individual projects which are subsequently co-ordinated at the centre (e.g., Creighton & Noyes, 1989; Creighton, 1992). This model is now being adopted by other agencies.

Collaboration on data collection by one agency could, of course, be extended to collaboration between agencies, with an undertaking to collect systematically the same 'core' information on all pre-defined group of cases.

As we noted in our Introduction, for both populations in the present study, the future has been described as bleak. Sexually abused children appear to be at risk of considerable adult distress and dysfunction; some go on to become sexual offenders themselves. A high proportion of young perpetrators continue their sexual aggression against both children and adults. Such conclusions have been based on retrospective studies of adults, the majority of whom received no therapy or intervention. We are in a position now to develop prospective studies of these two groups of children if child protection agencies and individual therapists grasp the issues we have raised. For the sake of the children and their families this opportunity must not be missed.

References

Abel, G. G., Becker, J. V., Mittelman, M., Rouleau, J. L., Murphy, W. D. (1987) Self-reported sex crimes of non-incarcerated paraphiliacs. Journal of Interpersonal Violence, **2(1)**, 3–25.

Achenbach, T. M. (1991) *Manual for the Child Behaviour Checklist/4–18 and 1991 Profile.* Burlington, V. T.: University of Vermont Department of Psychiatry.

Achenbach, T. M. & Edelbrock, C. (1983) *Manual for the Child Behaviour Checklist and revised Child Behaviour Profile.* Burlington, V. T.: University Associates in Psychiatry.

Alexander, P. C. & Lupfer, S. L. (1987) Family characteristics and long term consequences associated with sexual abuse. Archives of Sexual Behaviour, **16**, 235–245.

Baker, A. W. & Duncan, S. P. (1985) Child sexual abuse: a study of prevalence in Great Britain. Child Abuse & Neglect, **9**, 457–467.

Bannister, A. (1994) Journey of discovery. Community Care: Supplement 1023, 30 June–6 July, 1994 (page 5).

Beck, A. T., Ward, C. H., Mendelson, M., Mock, J. & Erbaugh, J. (1961) An inventory for measuring depression. Archives of General Psychiatry, **4**, 561–571.

Beck, A. T. & Steer, R. A. (1987) *Beck Depression Inventory Manual.* New York: The Psychological Corporation, Harcourt Brace Jovanovich, Inc.

Becker, J. V. (1990) Treating adolescent sex offenders. Professional Psychology: Research & Practice, **21(5)**, 362–365.

Becker, J. V., Kaplan, M. S. & Kavoussi, R. (1988) Measuring the effectiveness of treatment for the aggressive adolescent sexual offender. Annals of the New York Academy of Sciences, **528**, 215–222.

Beckett, R., Leek, C., O'Callaghan, D. & Print, B. (in preparation) A comparative study of adolescent sex offenders and non-sexual offenders in the UK.

Berliner, L. (1991) Clinical work with sexually abused children. In C. R. Hollins & K. Howells, (Eds), *Clinical Approaches to Sex Offenders and their Victims.* Chapter 9. Chichester, UK: John Wiley & Sons Ltd.

Briere, J. (1992) *Child abuse trauma: theory and treatment of lasting effects.* Newbury Park, CA: Sage.

Browne, K. (1993) Home visitation and child abuse: the British experience. The American Professional Society on the Abuse of Children Advisor, **6(4)**, 11–12, 28–31.

Cohen, P. The minefield: ouster orders. Community Care, Supplement: 30.6.94.

Cohen, J. A. & Mannarino, A. P. (1988) Psychological symptoms in sexually abused girls. Child Abuse & Neglect, **12**, 571–577.

Conte, J. R., Berliner, L. & Schuerman, J. (1986) The impact of sexual abuse on children. Final Technical Report NIMH grant no. MH37133, Department of HHS, Washington, DC.

Creighton, S. (1992) *Child abuse trends in England and Wales 1988–1990*. London: National Society for the Prevention of Cruelty to Children.

Creighton, S. & Noyes, P. (1989) *Child abuse trends in England & Wales 1983–1987*. London: NSPCC.

Department of Health (1995) Child protection: messages from research. HMSO.

Dobson, R. (1994) Children should be seen and heard. Community Care, 1025, 14–15.

Dubowitz, H., Black, M. & Hartington, D. (1992) The diagnosis of child sexual abuse. American Journal of Diseases in Childhood, **146(6)**, 688–693.

Everson, M. D., Hunter, W. M. & Runyan, D. K. (1991). Adolescent adjustment after incest: who fares poorly? Paper presented at the San Diego Conference on Responding to Child Maltreatment, San Diego, CA.

Finkelhor, D. (1979) *Sexually victimised children*. New York: Free Press.

Finkelhor, D. & Berliner, L. (1995) Research on the treatment of sexually abused children: a review and recommendations. Journal of the American Academy of Child & Adolescent Psychiatry, **34**, 1–16.

Friedlander, S., Weiss, D. S. & Taylor, J. (1986) Assessing the influence of maternal depression on the validity of the Child Behaviour Checklist. Journal of Abnormal Child Psychology, **14**, 123–133.

Furby, L., Weinrott, M. R. & Blackshaw, L. (1989) Sex offender recidivism: a review. Psychological Bulletin, **105(1)**, 3–30.

Gibbons, J., Conroy, S. & Bell, C. (1995a) Operating the Child Protection system: a study in child protection practices in English Local Authorities. HMSO.

Gibbons, J., Gallagher, B., Bell, C., & Gordon, D. (1995b) Development after physical abuse in early childhood: a follow-up study of children on Protective Registers. HMSO.

Giller, H., Gormley, C. & Williams, P. (1992) The effectiveness of the Child Protection procedures: an evaluation of Child Protection procedures in four ACPC areas. London: Social Information Systems.

Glasgow, D., Horne, L., Calam, R. & Cox, A. (1994) Evidence, incidence, gender and age in sexual abuse of children perpetrated by children. Child Abuse Review, **3**, 196–210.

Goldberg, D. P. & Hiller, V. F. (1979) A scaled version of the General Health Questionnaire. Psychological Medicine, **9**, 139–145.

Gomes-Schwartz, B., Horowitz, J. M. & Cardarelli, A. P., (1990) *Child sexual abuse: the initial effects*. Newbury Park, CA: Sage.

Goodman, G. S., Taub, E. P., Jones, D. P. H., England, P., Port, L. K., Rudy, L. & Prado, L. (1992). Testifying in criminal courts: emotional effects on child sexual assault victims. Monographs of the Society for Research in Child Development, **57** (**5**, serial no: 229), 1–159.

Gray, E. (1993) *Unequal justice: the prosecution of child sexual abuse*. New York: The Free Press.

Gudjonsson, G. H. & Singh, K. K. (1989) The revised Gudjonsson Blame Attribution Inventory. Personality & Individual Differences, **5**, 53–58.

Gudjonsson, G. H. & Petursson, H. (1991) The attribution of blame and type of crime committed: transcultural validation. Journal of the Forensic Science Society, **31**, 349–352.

Harter, S. (1985) The self-perception profile for children. Denver, CO: University of Denver.

Harter, S. (1987) The self-perception profile for adolescents. Denver, CO: University of Denver.

Home Office (1992) Criminal statistics for England & Wales 1992. London: HMSO.

Hughes, B. & Parker, H. (1994) Save the children. Community Care, 1006, 24–25.

Hunter, J. A. & Santos, D. R. (1990) The use of specialised cognitive-behavioural therapies in the treatment of adolescent sex offenders. International Journal of Offender Therapy & Comparative Criminology, **34(3)**, 239–247.

Huxley, P. (1994) Outcome measurement in work with children: comparing plans in the UK with experience in the US. Child Abuse Review, **3**, 120–133.

Kahn, T. J. & Chambers, H. (1991) Assessing re-offence risk with juvenile sex offenders. Child Welfare, LXX(3).

Kahn, T. J. & Lafond, M. A. (1988) Treatment of the adolescent sex offender. Child & Adolescent Social Work Journal, **5**.

Kearney, P & Miller D. (1994) The numbers game. Community Care, 999, 22–23.

Kelly, L., Regan, L. & Burton, S. (1995) *An exploratory study of the prevalence of sexual abuse in a sample of 16–21 year olds*. London: HMSO.

Kendall-Tackett, K. A., Williams, L. M. & Finkelhor, D. (1993) Impact of sexual abuse on children: a review and synthesis of recent empirical studies. Psychological Bulletin, **113**, 164–180.

Kingsbury, S. J. (1993) Parasuicide in adolescence: a message in a bottle. ACPP Review & Newsletter, 15(6), 253–259. London: Association of Child Psychology & Psychiatry.

Knopp, F. H., Freeman Longo, R. & Stevenson, W. F. (1992) *Nationwide survey of juvenile and adult sex offender treatment programs and models*. Orwell, V. T.: Safer Society Program Publications.

Kovacs, M. & Beck A. T. (1977) An empirical clinical approach towards a definition of childhood depression. Schulterbrandt, J. G. & Raskin A. (Eds), *Depression in children: diagnosis, treatment and conceptual models*. New York: Raven Press.

Koverola, C., Pound, J., Heger, A., & Lytle, C. (1993) Relationship of child sexual abuse to depression. Child Abuse & Neglect, **17(3)**, 393–400.

Lonnqvist, J. (1984) Evaluation of psychiatric treatment. Psychiatria Fennica, **15**, 29–40.

McCune, N. Adolescent perpetrators of sexual abuse—longterm outcome of treatment. (Submitted for publication.)

Monck, E., Sharland, E., Bentovim, A., Goodall, G., Hyde, C. & Lwin, R. (1996). Descriptive and treatment outcome studies of families with a diagnosis of child sexual abuse. London HMSO.

Mullen, P. E., Martin, J. L., Anderson, J. C., Romans, S. E. & Herbison, G. P. (1993) Childhood sexual abuse and mental health in adult life. British Journal of Psychiatry, **163**, 721–732.

Murphy, W. D., Haynes, M. R. & Worley, P. J. (1991) Assessment of adult sexual interest. In C. R. Hollin & K. Howells (Eds), *Clinical approaches to sex offenders and their victims*. Chichester, UK: John Wiley & Sons.

Myers, J. E. B. (1993) A call for forensically relevant research. *Child Abuse & Neglect*, **17**, 573–579.

National Adolescent Perpetrator Network (1988) Preliminary report from the National Task Force on Juvenile Sexual Offending. Juvenile & Family Court Journal, **39(2)**.

NCH Action for Children (1992) *The report of the committee of enquiry into children and young people who sexually abuse other children*. London: NCH Action for Children.

National Research Council (1993) *Understanding child abuse and neglect*. Washington, DC: National Academy Press.

Newman, T. (1994) quoted in Community Care, 1008, 17.3.94, page 14.

Noyes, P. (1993) quoted in Community Care, No. 989, 21 October.

O'Callaghan, D. & Print, B. (1994) Adolescent sex abusers: research, assessment and treatment. In A. Morrison, M. Erooga & R. C. Beckett (Eds), *Sexual offending against children: assessment and treatment of male abusers*. Chapter 7, 146–177. London: Routledge.

Ollendick, T. H. (1993) Reliability and validity of the Fear Survey Schedule for Children—Revised (FSSC-R). Behaviour Research and Therapy, **21**, 685–692.

Ollendick, T. H. Yule, W. & Ollier, K. (1991) Fears in British children and their relationship to manifest anxiety and depression. Journal of Child Psychology & Psychiatry, **32**, 321–331.

OPCS (Office of Population Censuses and Surveys) 1989. General Household Survey, p 10. HMSO.

Pietrzak, J., Ramler, M., Renner, T., Ford, L., & Gilbert, N. (1990) *Practical Problem Evaluation: examples from child abuse prevention*. Newbury Park, CA: Sage.

Plotkinoff, J. & Woolfson, R. (1994) quoted in Community Care 1009, 24.3.94.

Research Team, The (1990) *Child sexual abuse in Northern Ireland*. Antrim, NI: Greystone Books.

Ross, J. & Loss, P. (1991) Assessment of the juvenile sex offender. In G. Ryan & S. Lane (Eds), *Juvenile sexual offending: causes, consequences and correction*. Massachusetts: Lexington Books.

Rubinstein, M., Yeager, C. A., Goodstein, C. & Lewis, D. O. (1993) Sexually assaultive male juveniles: a follow-up. American Journal of Psychiatry, **150(2)**, 262–265.

Russell, D. E. H. (1996) *The Secret Trauma: incest in the lives of girls and women*. New York: Basic Books.

Ryan, G. & Lane, S. (1991) *Juvenile sexual offending: causes, consequences and correction.* Lexington, MT: Lexington Books.

Shaffer, D. & Piacentini, J. (1994) Suicide and attempted suicide. In M. Rutter, E. Taylor & L. Hersov. (Eds), *Child & Adolescent Psychiatry: modern approaches.* Oxford: Blackwell Publications.

Sharland, E., Jones, D., Aldgate, J., Seal, H. & Croucher, M. (in preparation) Professional Intervention in Child Sexual Abuse. HMSO.

Smith, G. (1994) Parent, partner, protector: conflicting role demands for mothers of sexually abused children. In A. Morrison, M. Erooga & R. C. Beckett (Eds), *Sexual offending against children: assessment and treatment of male abusers.* Chapter 8, 178–202. London: Routledge.

Smith, M. & Bentovim, A. (1994) Sexual Abuse. In M. Rutter, E. Taylor & L. Hersov. (Eds), *Child & Adolescent Psychiatry: modern approaches.* Oxford: Blackwell Publications.

Sone, K. (1994) Honesty pays off: review of Rochdale child protection. Community Care, 1027, 24.

Social Services Inspectorate (1994) Evaluating child protection services: findings and issues. Inspections of six local authority child protection services 1993: Overview Report. London: HMSO.

Stevenson, J. (1986) Evaluation studies of psychological treatment of children and practical constraints on their design. Newsletter: Association of Child Psychology & Psychiatry, **8(2)**, 2–11.

Stevenson, J., Batten, N., & Cherner, M. (1992) Fears and fearfulness in children and adolescents: a genetic study of twins data. Journal of Child Psychology & Psychiatry, 33(6), 977–985.

Taylor, E. A. & Stansfield, S. A. (1984) Children who poison themselves. British Journal of Psychiatry, 145, 127–135.

Thorpe, D. (1994) Facing Reality. Community Care, 1010, 32–33.

Tjaden, P. G. & Thoennes, N. (1992) Predictors of legal intervention in child maltreatment cases. Child Abuse & Neglect, 16, 807–821.

Tong, L., Oates, K. & McDowell, M. (1987) Personality development following sexual abuse. Child Abuse & Neglect, **11**, 371–383.

van Scoyk, S., Gray, J., & Jones, D. P.H. (1988) A theoretical framework for evaluation and treatment of the victims of child sexual assault by a nonfamily member. Family Process, 27, 105–113.

Vizard, E., Monck, E. & Misch, P. (1995) Child and adolescent sex abuse perpetrators: a review of the research literature. Journal of Child Psychology & Psychiatry, **36(5)**, 731–756.

Wagner, W. G. (1991) Depression in mothers of sexually abused vs. mothers of non-abused children. Child Abuse & Neglect, **15(1–2)**, 99–104.

Watkins, B. & Bentovim, A. (1992) Sexual abuse of male children and adolescents. Journal of Child Psychology & Psychiatry, **33**, 197–248.

Wasserman, J. & Kappel, S. (1985) Adolescent sex offenders in Vermont. Burlington, VT: Department of Health.

Waterman, J. (1993) Mediators of effects on children: what enhances optimal functioning and promotes healing? In J. Waterman, R. J. Kelly, J. McCord & M. K. Oliveri (Eds), *Behind the playground walls: sexual abuse in pre-schools.* New York: Guilford Press.

Waterman, J. & Lusk, R. (1993) Psychological testing in evaluation of child sexual abuse. Child Abuse & Neglect, **17(1)**, 145–159.

Wiffen, J. (1994) quoted in Community Care, 1008, 17.3.94, page 14.

Will, D. (1995) A treatment service for adolescent sex offenders: the first 50 referrals.

Williams, B. T. R. & Santry, S. Section 53: Sex offenders (submitted for publication). Behavioural Science Unit, Institute of Child Health, London.

Appendix A

The Treatment Centres

National Society for the Prevention of Cruelty to Children (NSPCC)

i)   Stockport:
ii) Gloucester and Border Counties Child Protection Team (CPT):
iii) Tyne & Wear:
iv) Craigavon; N. Ireland:
v)   Derby CPT:
vi) Croydon CPT:

Family Service Units (FSU)

i)   South London:
ii) Bradford:
iii) East Leeds:
iv) Leicester:

National Children's Home (NCH)

i)   Port Talbot; Wales:
ii) Ipswich:
iii) Ashford, Kent:
iv) Sunderland:
v)   Nottingham:
vi   West Cumbria, Whitehaven:

Northorpe Hall Trust

i)   Northorpe Hall, West Yorks

St Christopher's Fellowship

i)   Howard House

Appendix B

The number of young perpetrators entering treatment programmes and the research project.

Centres	Number in follow-up study
Craigavon NSPCC	10
Belfast Young People's Centre	10
Leicester FSU	14
Bradford FSU	8
Stockport NSPCC	4
Tyne & Wear NSPCC	4
Ipswich NCH/Action for Children	1
Port Talbot/Action for Children	1
Northorpe Hall	1
Croydon NSPCC	1
W. Cumbria NCH/Action for Children	1

Appendix C(a): Example of consent form for Parents of sexually abused children

The Family Health Study
Institute of Child Health, London WC1N 1EH
tel: 071–831–0975
Howard House, 30 Belsize Avenue, London NW3

Parents' Consent Form

I am the parent (or guardian) of _____

I have had the purpose of the Family Health Study explained to me, and I understand that all information I give to the researchers will be confidential.

I am willing/unwilling* to fill in some short questionnaires about my child to help the research.

Signed . . . .   Date . . . .

Parent's name
(BLOCK CAPITALS PLEASE) _____

Address _____

_____

_____

[This form will be held by Howard House andd we will tell the research team that you have given your consent: the research team will not know your name or address.]

I agree to let Howard House contact my child's school or playgroup IN CONFIDENCE to obtain information

about how well _____ is doing there.

Signed _____   Date _____

Name of school/playgroup _____

Appendix C(b): Example of Information sheet for parents of sexually abused children

The Family Health Study
Institute of Child Health, London WC1N 1EH
tel: 071–831–0975
Leicester FSU, 26 Severn Street, Leicester, LE2 0NN
tel: (0533) 543–352

Information on the Study

Many of the children and teenagers who are sexually abused need help to get over the effects of the abuse. Families need help as well, sometimes to recover from the shock of discovery, sometimes to learn how to help their child.

We are trying to find ways of improving the help which the children and their families receive after the discovery of sexual abuse.

Our study is designed to obtain a picture of how the children and teenagers are before their treatment starts in the Leicester Family Service Unit and then again after 12 months. That way we will be able to tell what effect the treatment has had, and just how much better the children and families are feeling.

This is not the only treatment centre involved in this study. At the end of the year we will also be able to find out if one sort of treatment is better than another, or whether they are all as helpful as each other. This is what we expect to find.

While your child/teenager is attending Leicester FSU we will be asking you to join in this research project. This will mean that we ask you to give us some information about how your child is behaving and feeling; we will ask for this once at the start of treatment and once 12 months later. At the end of 12 months we will also ask you to tell us what your feelings are about the helpfulness of the treatment.

AT ALL TIMES the information which you or anyone else gives us about your child or family will be held in COMPLETE CONFIDENCE.

If you have any questions about the research please do not hesitate to ring us on one of the numbers at the top of the page, or talk, to the project co-ordinator at FSU.

With thanks for your help with this important research.

Elizabeth Monck
Senior Researcher

Gordon Punshon
FSU Unit Organiser

Appendix C(c): Example of consent form for parents of young perpetrators

The Family Health Study
Institute of Child Health, London WC1N 1EH
tel: 071–831–0975
Leicester FSU, 26 Severn Street, Leicester

Parents' Consent Form

I am the parent (or guardian) of _____

I have had the purpose of the Family Health Study explained to me, and I understand that all information I give to the researchers will be confidential.

I am willing/unwilling★ to fill in some short questionnaires about my son/foster son to help the research.

Signed . . . .   Date . . . .

Parent's/guardian's name
(BLOCK CAPITALS PLEASE) _____

Address _____

_____

_____

[This form will be held by Leicester FSU and we will tell the research team that you have given your consent: the research team will not know your name or address.]

I agree to let Leicester FSU contact my child's school or college IN CONFIDENCE to obtain information

about how well _____ is doing there.

Signed _____   Date _____

Name of school _____

Address _____

_____

Name of teacher/tutor to contact _____
★ delete as necessary

Appendix C(d): Example of Information sheet for parents of young perpetrators

The Family Health Study
Institute of Child Health, London WC1N 1EH
tel: 071–831–0975
Leicester FSU, 26 Severn Street, Leicester, LE2 0NN
tel: (0533) 543–352

Information on the Study

It is well known that the teenagers and young men who are involved in abusive behaviour towards other children need a lot of help to break away from that behaviour. Families need help as well, sometimes to recover from the shock of discovery, sometimes to learn how to help their child.

We are trying to find ways of improving the help which these young men and their families receive after the discovery of sexual abuse.

Our study is designed to obtain a picture of how the teenagers and young men are before their treatment starts in the Leicester Family Service Unit, and then again after 12 months. That way we will be able to tell what effect the treatment has had.

This is not the only treatment centre involved in this study. At the end of the year we will also be able to find out if one sort of treatment is better than another, or whether they are all as helpful as each other. This is what we expect to find.

While your son is attending the Leicester FSU we will be asking you to join in this research project by giving us some information about how your son is behaving and feeling; we will ask for this once at the start of treatment and once 12 months later. At the end of 12 months we will also ask you to tell us what your feelings are about the helpfulness of the treatment.

AT ALL TIMES the information which you or anyone else gives us about your child or family will be held in COMPLETE CONFIDENCE.

If you have any questions about the research please do not hesitate to ring us on one of the numbers at the top of the page, or talk, to the project co-ordinator at FSU.

With thanks for your help with this important research.

Elizabeth Monck   Gordon Punshon
Senior Researcher   FSU Unit Organiser

Appendix D

Classification of the types of abusive action by the young perpetrators.

1 Exhibitionism
2 Inspects victm's genitals/little or no touching
3 Forces victim to view adult sexual actions
4 Fondling, inappropriate touching
5 Masturbation of victim by perpetrator
6 Masturbation of perpetrator by victim
7 Genital to genital contact—unclothed
8 Perpetrator performs cunnilingus on victim
9 Perpetrator performs fellatio on victim
10 Victim performs cunnilingus on perpetrator
11 Victim performs fellatio on perpetrator
12 Perpetrator attempts anal intercourse
13 Perpetrator attempts vaginal intercourse
14 Digital penetration
15 Anal intercourse
16 Vaginal intercourse
17 Using victim in pornography
18 Showing victim sexually inappropriate video/film

Printed in the United Kingdom for HMSO
Dd301191 1/96 C10 G559 10170